YET ANOTHER MOM
COLORING BOOK

SIMPLE SYMMETRY
VOLUME 1

MANDALAS & MORE

designed and illustrated by

Cynthia Caldwell

Printed in the USA.

First Edition

ISBN: 978-0-9968638-0-3

Symmetry is all around us. You find it in your home, in nature, in science, in life. It can have a very calming effect on us, easing our minds, telling us that everything is in its place; everything is where it should be.

Coloring symmetrical patterns, especially the circular designs of mandalas, can help you focus and release stress. As you color, you tune out the chaos of life and find relaxation and peace in the simple act of putting color to paper.

But one very important reminder: be sure to remember the reason you bought this book! Do NOT allow yourself to stress out about color choices, or going outside the lines, or mistakes in a pattern. There are no judges here! Just say what my 6-year-old daughter says when she falls or spills or makes a mistake: "I meant to do that!"

I hope you enjoy the designs I have created here for you. Some of them have simple, easily recognizable patterns, while some may look haphazard and chaotic. But there really is a pattern to be found in all of these designs. Just don't stress out if you cannot figure out the pattern. Color it random!

Now go get your crayons, pencils, pens, or whatever, and start coloring!

P.S. Please visit my web site Yet Another Mom (yetanothermom.com) for free coloring page downloads, coloring tips, colored samples of these designs, my blog and more. And I'd love to see your finished creations!

This book is dedicated to my daughter Emma,
for if it hadn't been for her, I would not have
started coloring again as an adult!

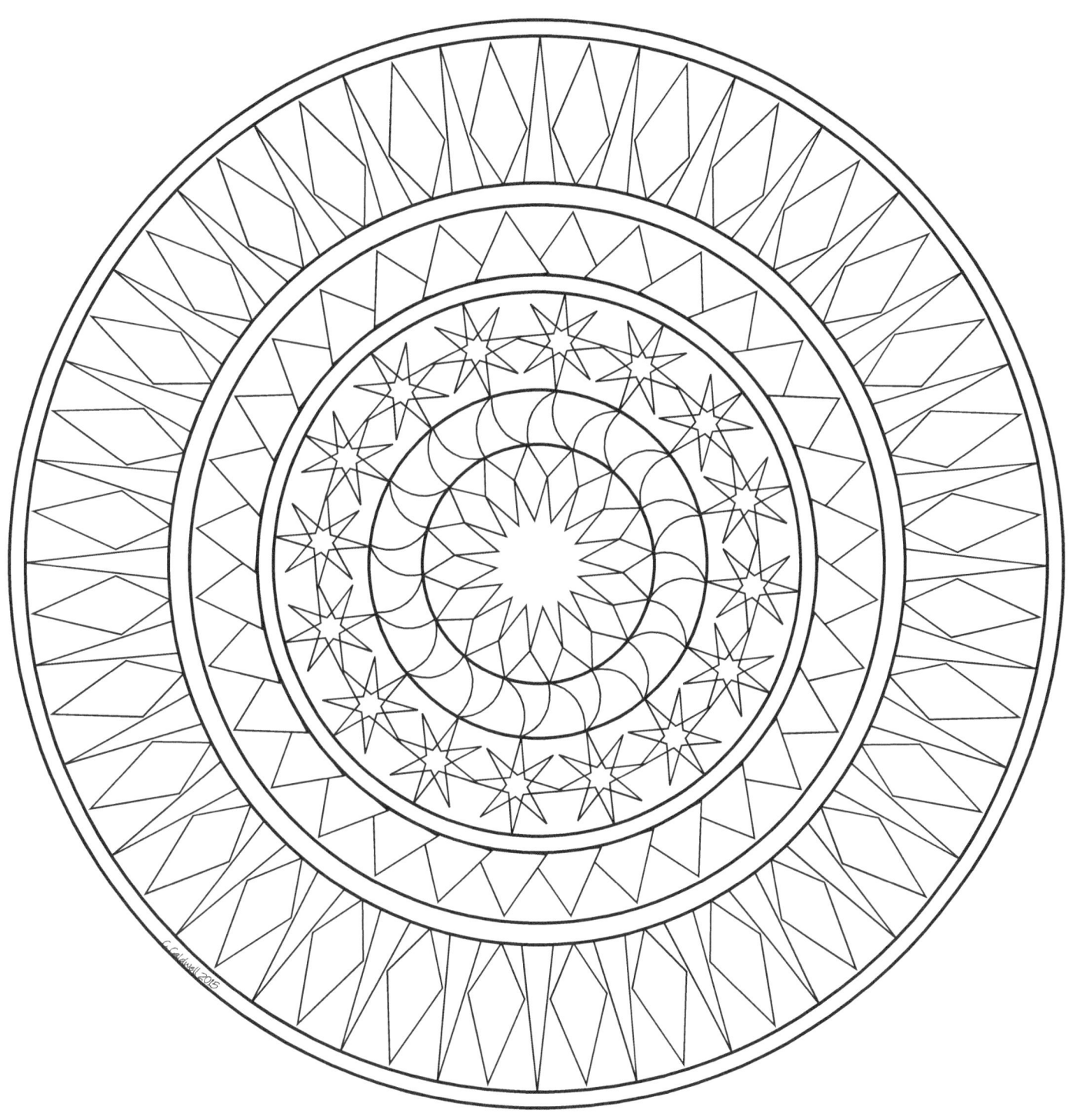

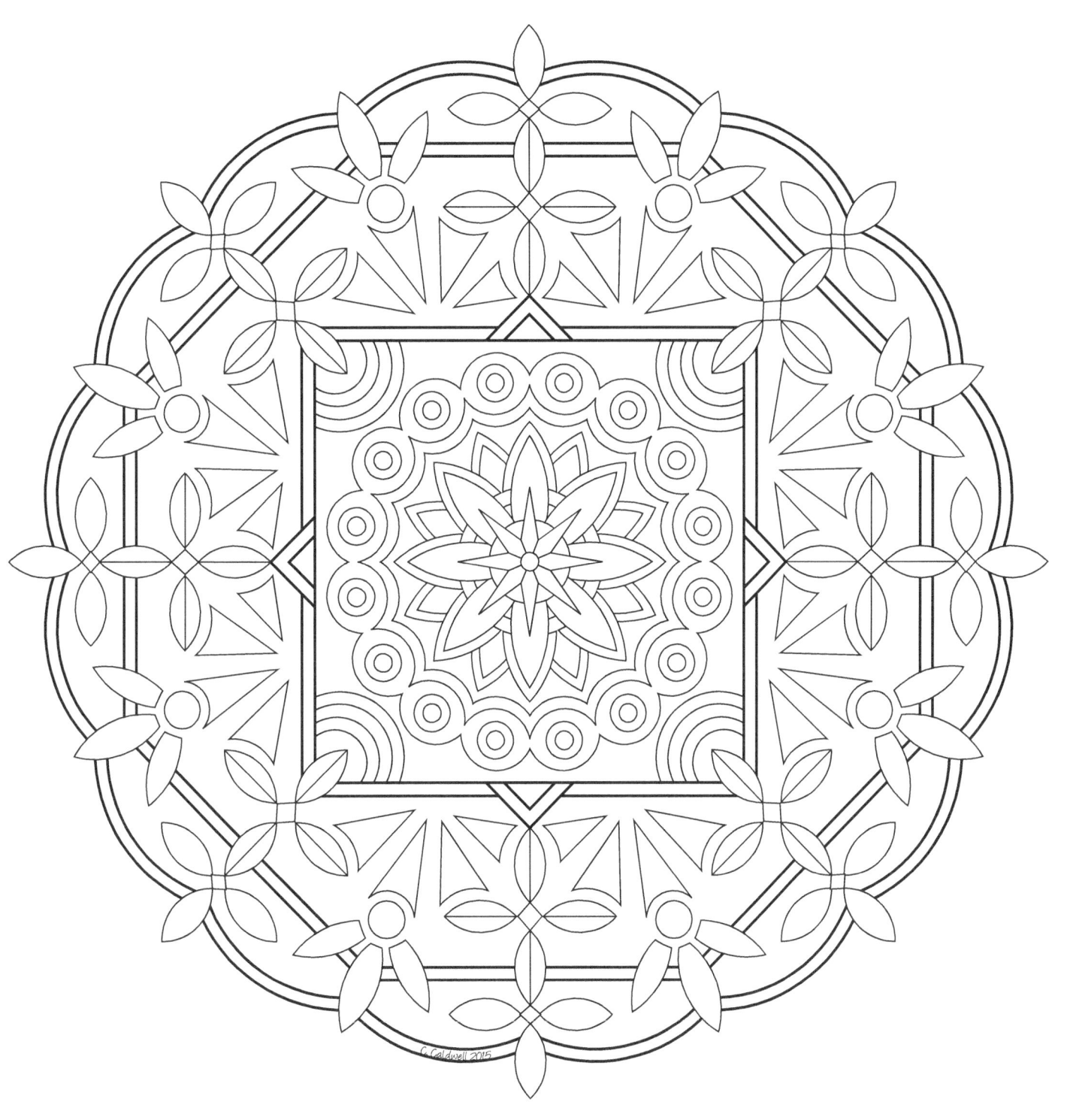

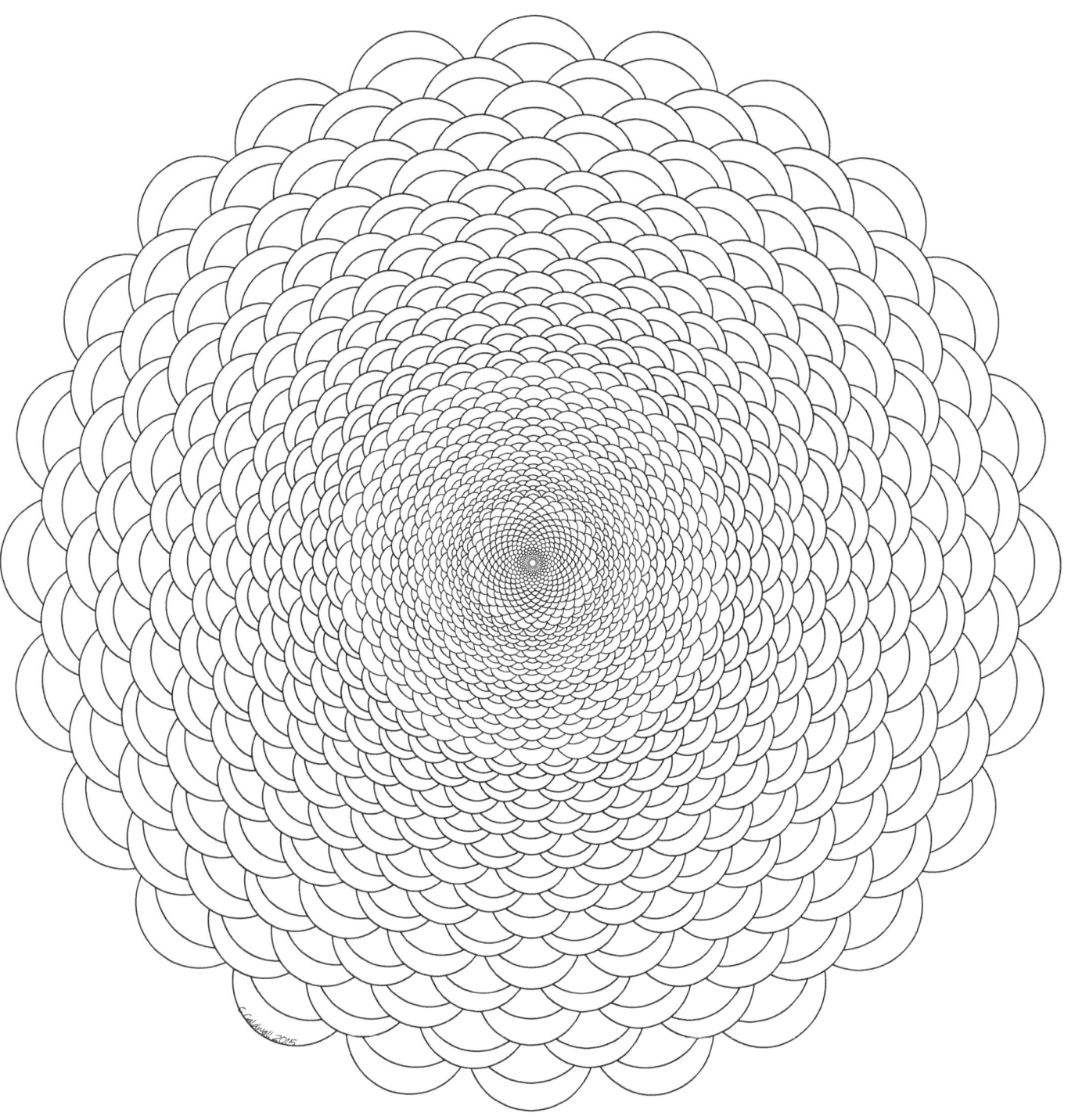

YET ANOTHER MOM COLORING BOOK
SIMPLE SYMMETRY, VOLUME 1
MANDALAS & MORE

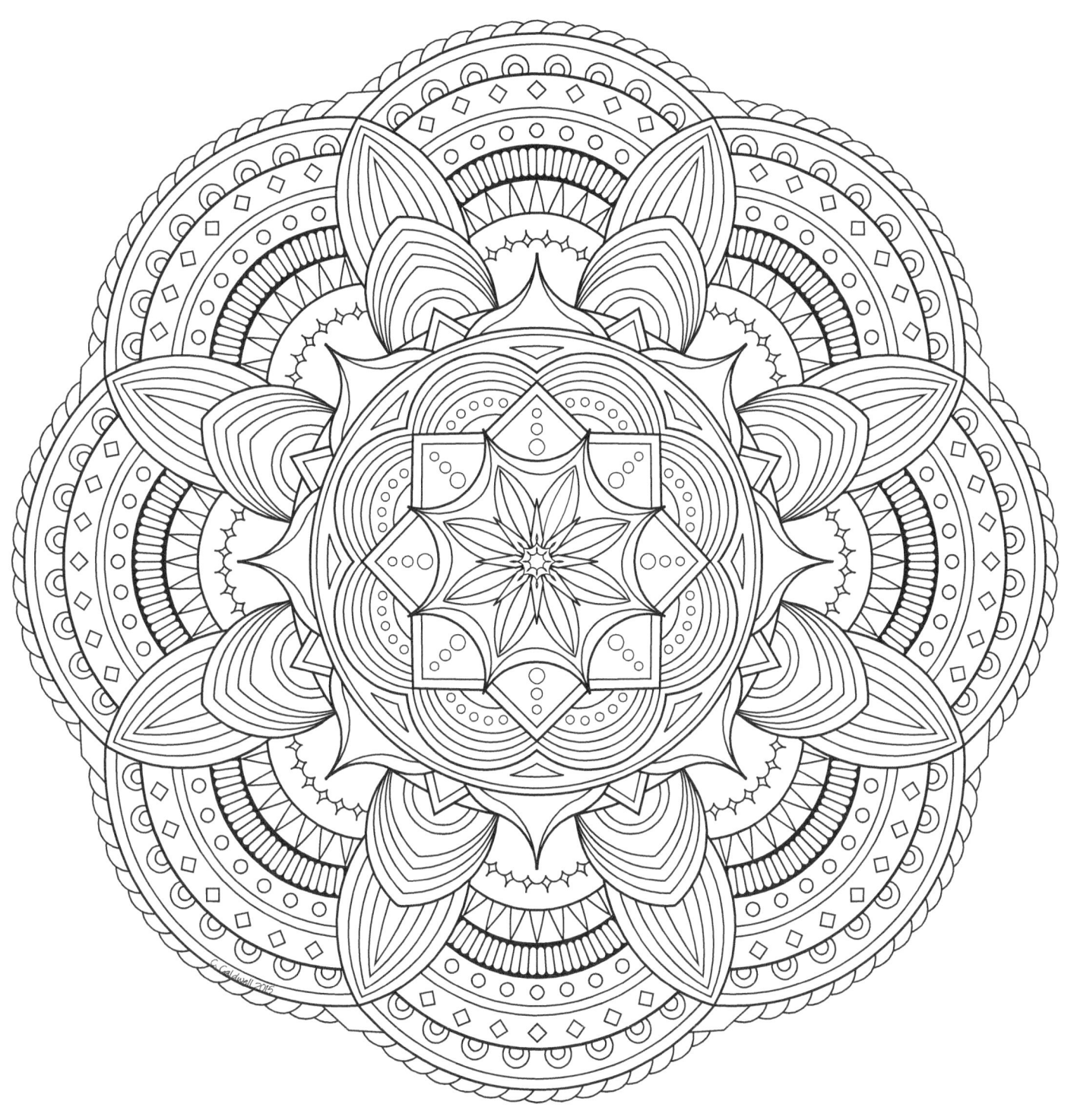

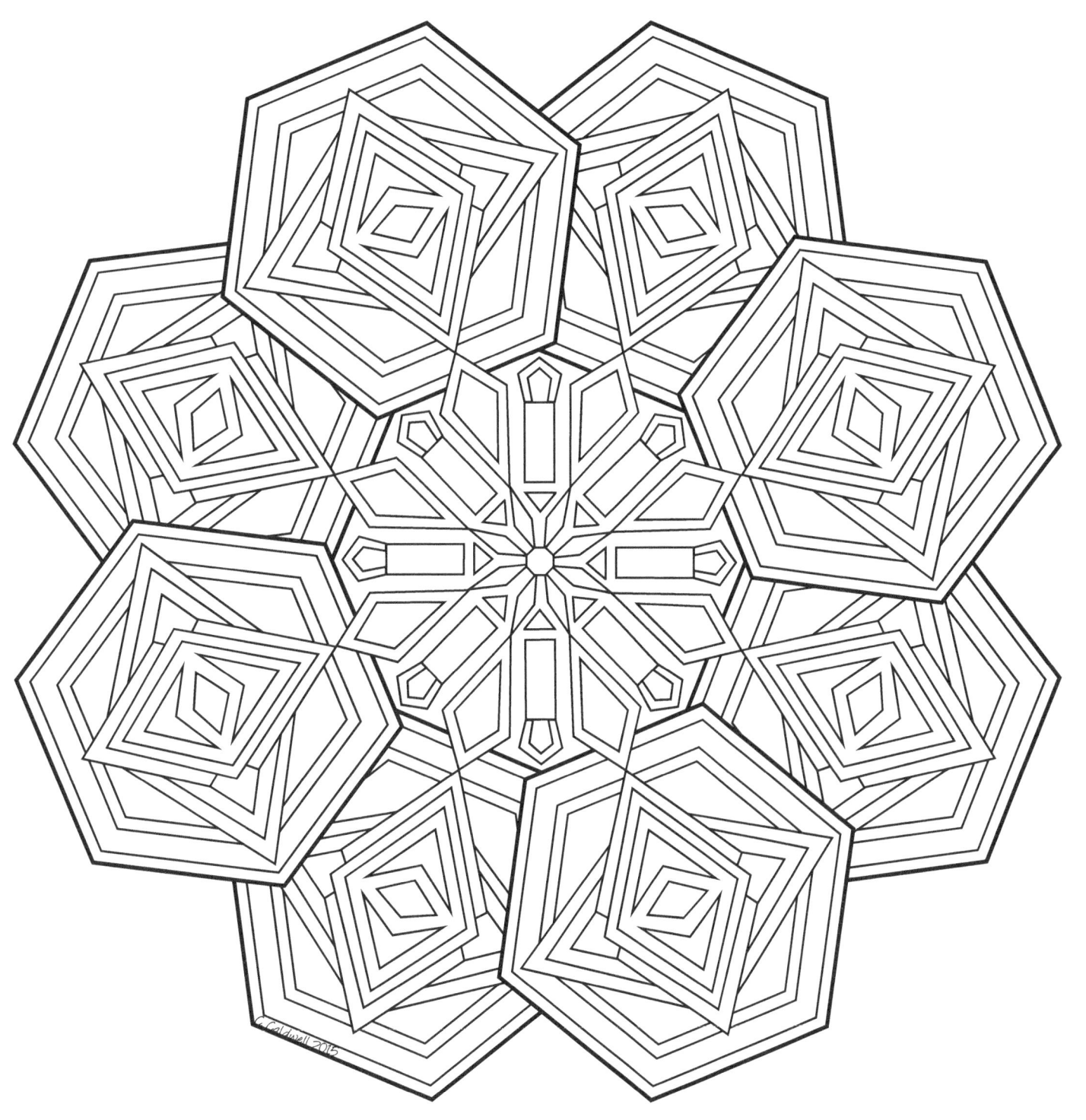

C Caldwell 2015

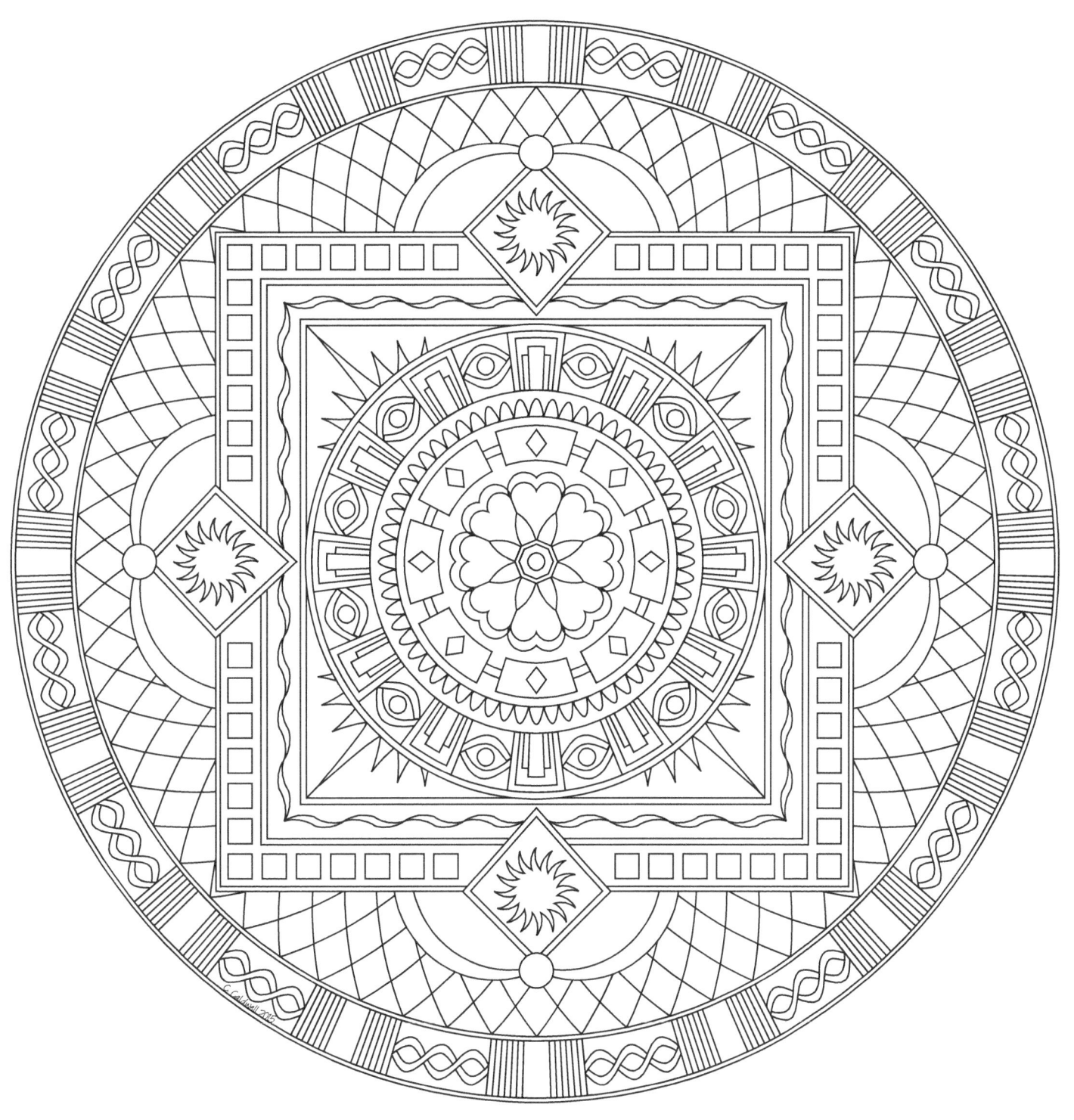

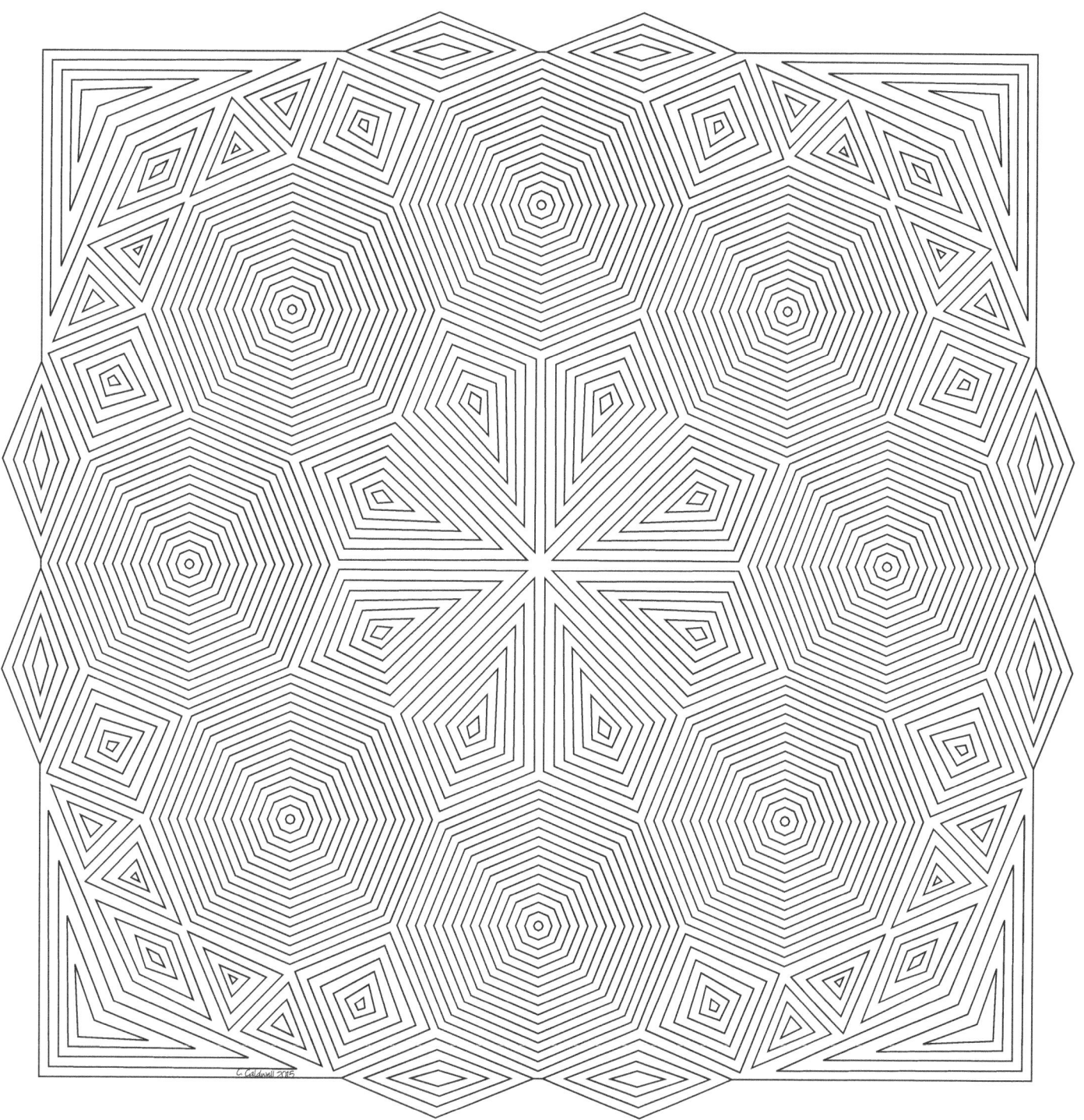

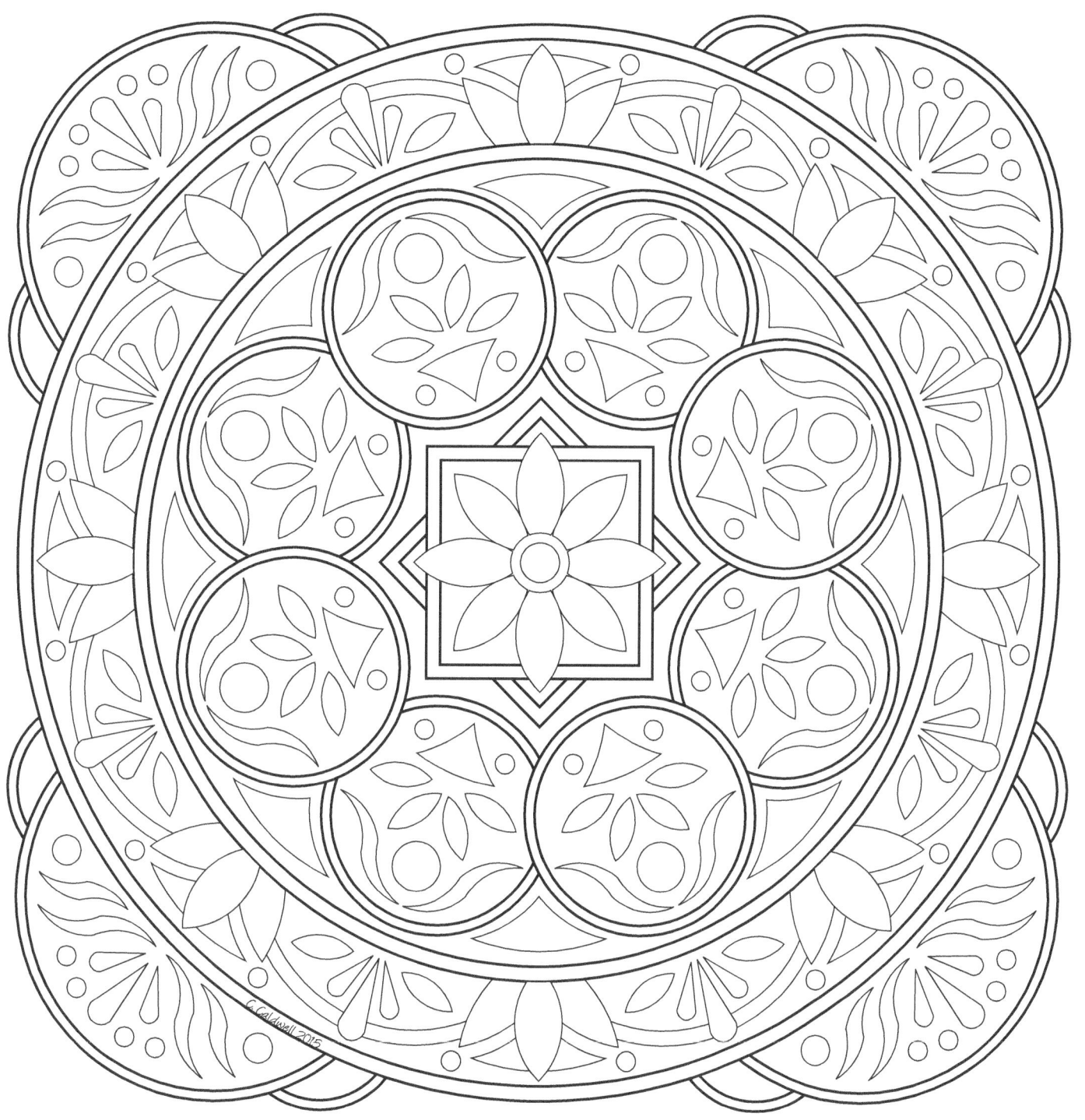

C. Caldwell 2015

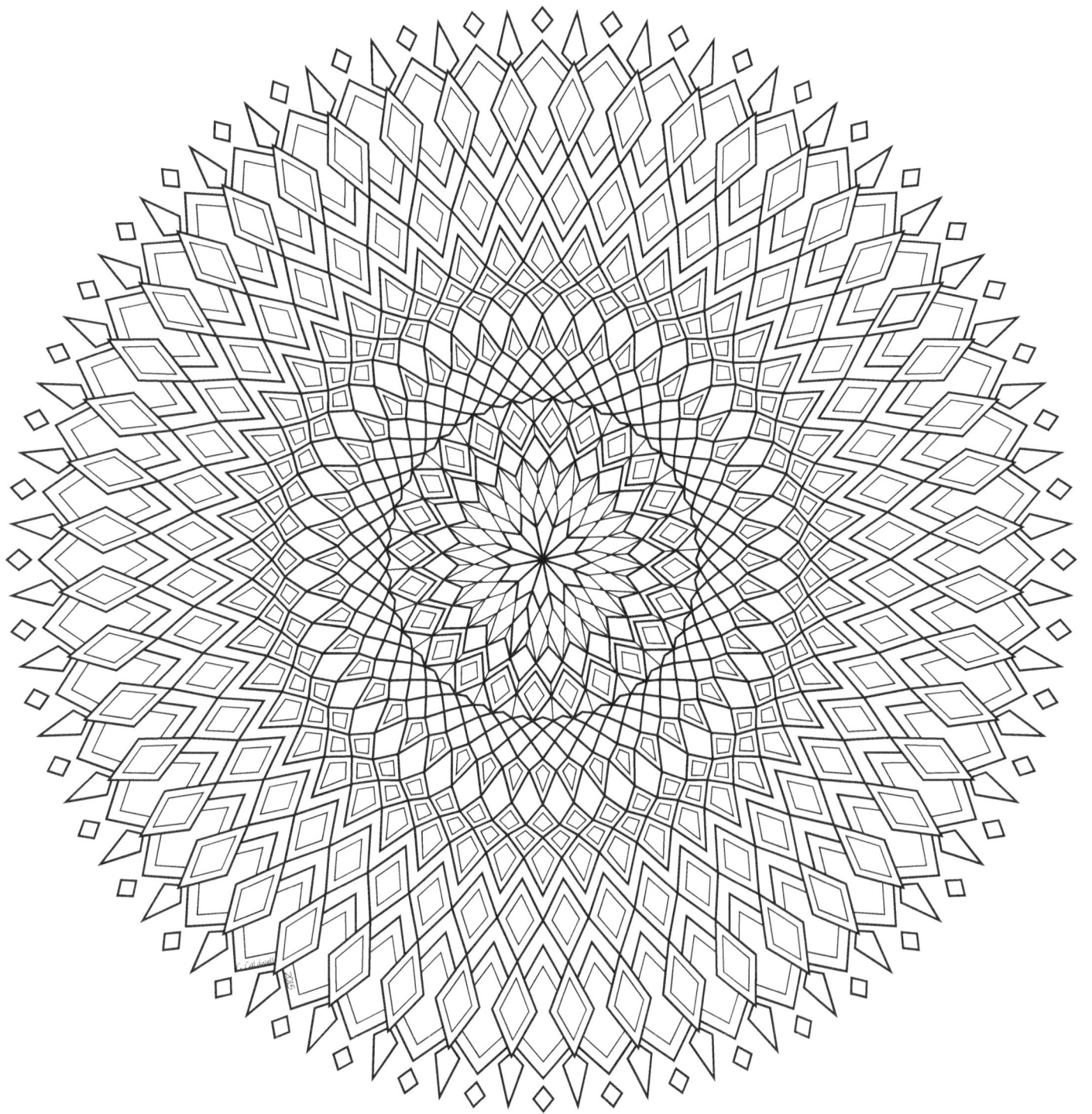

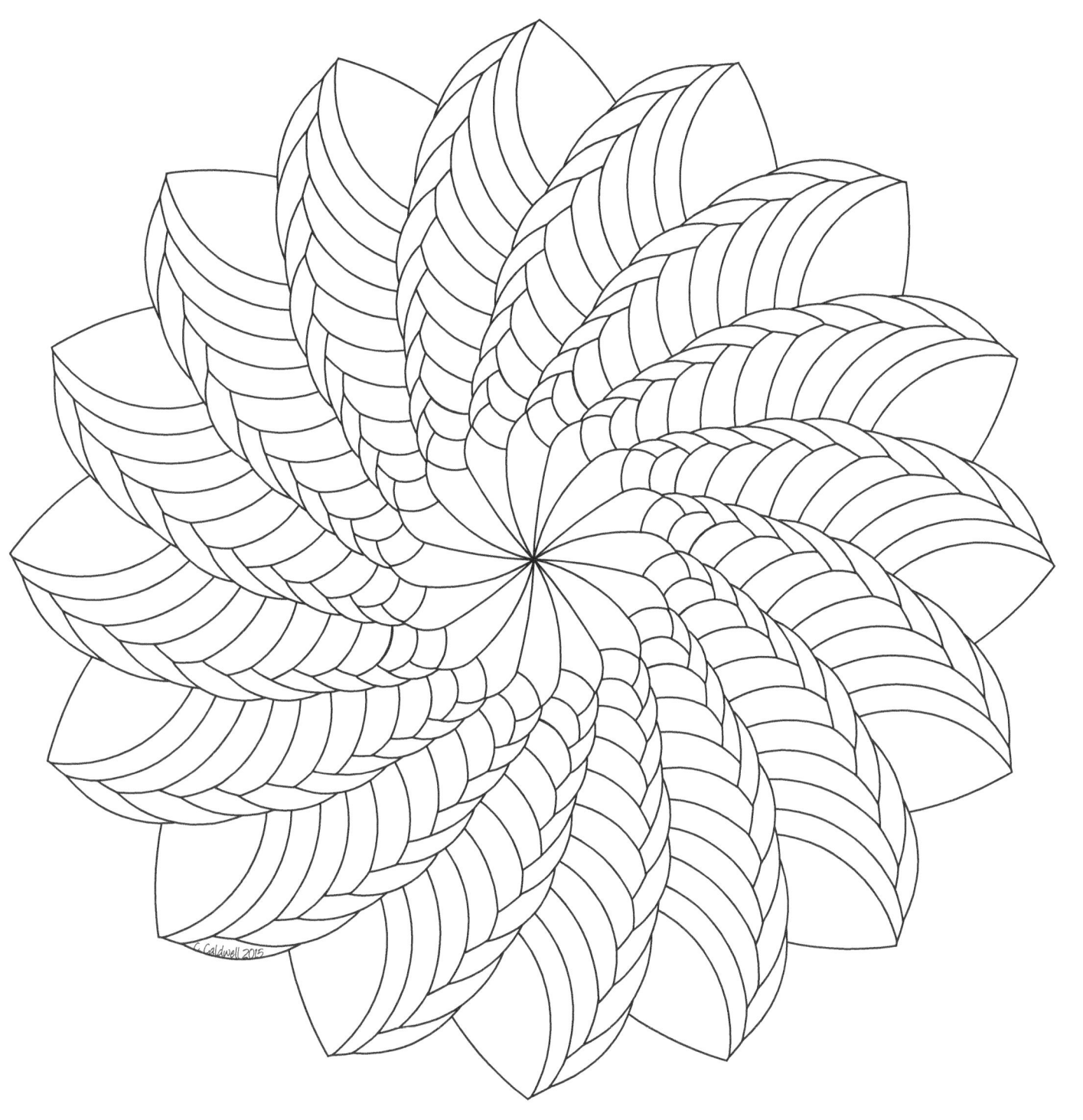

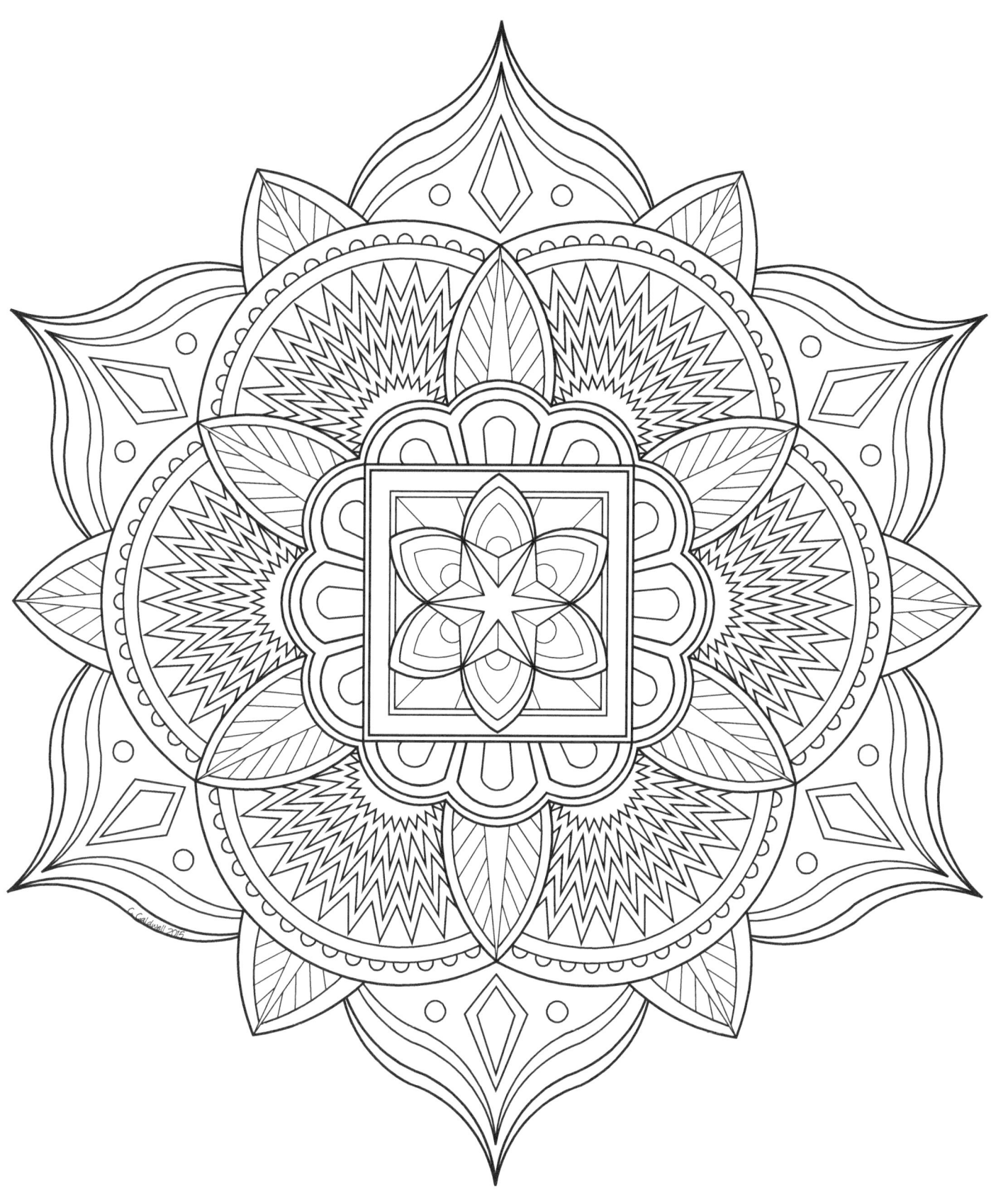

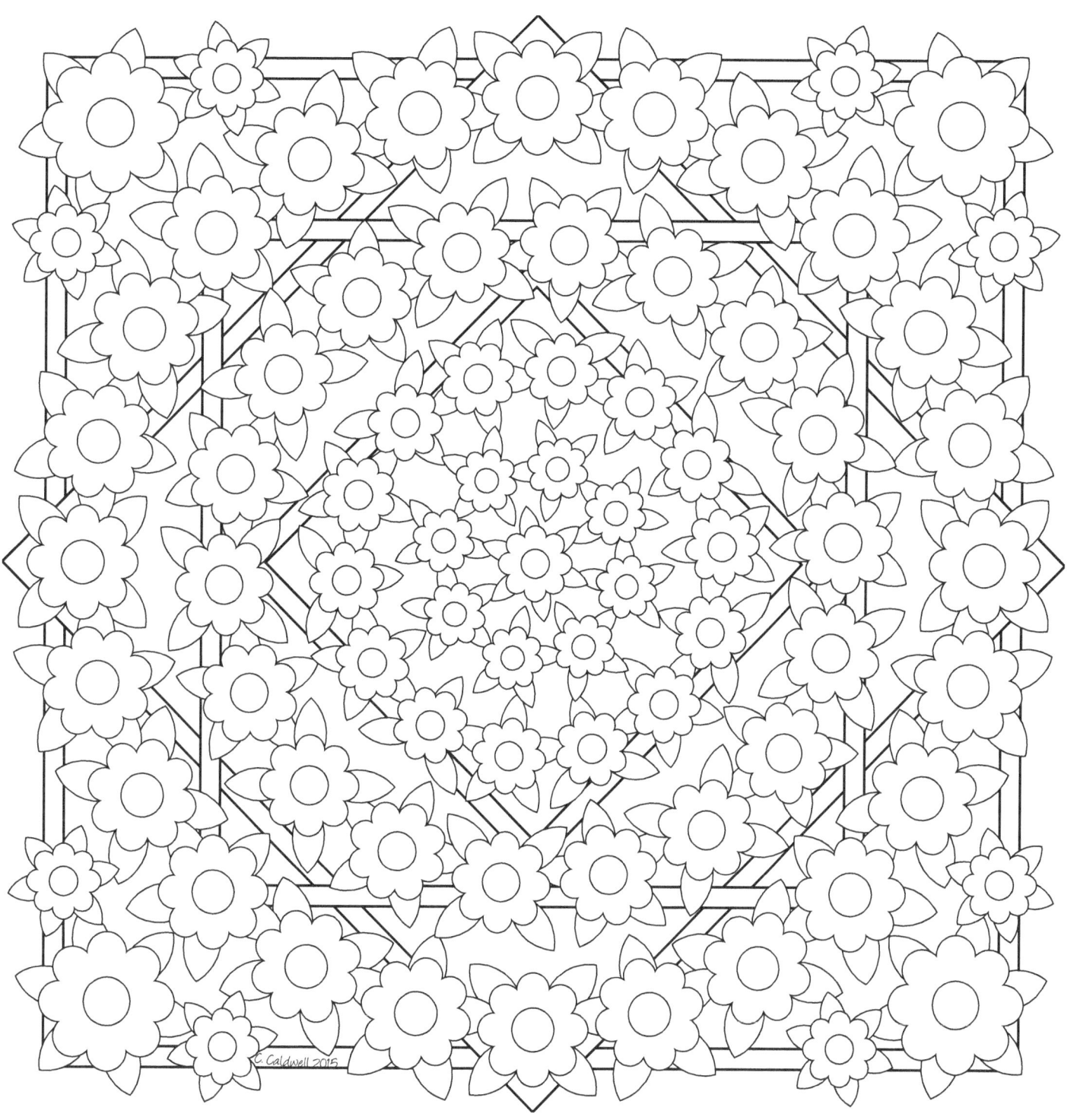

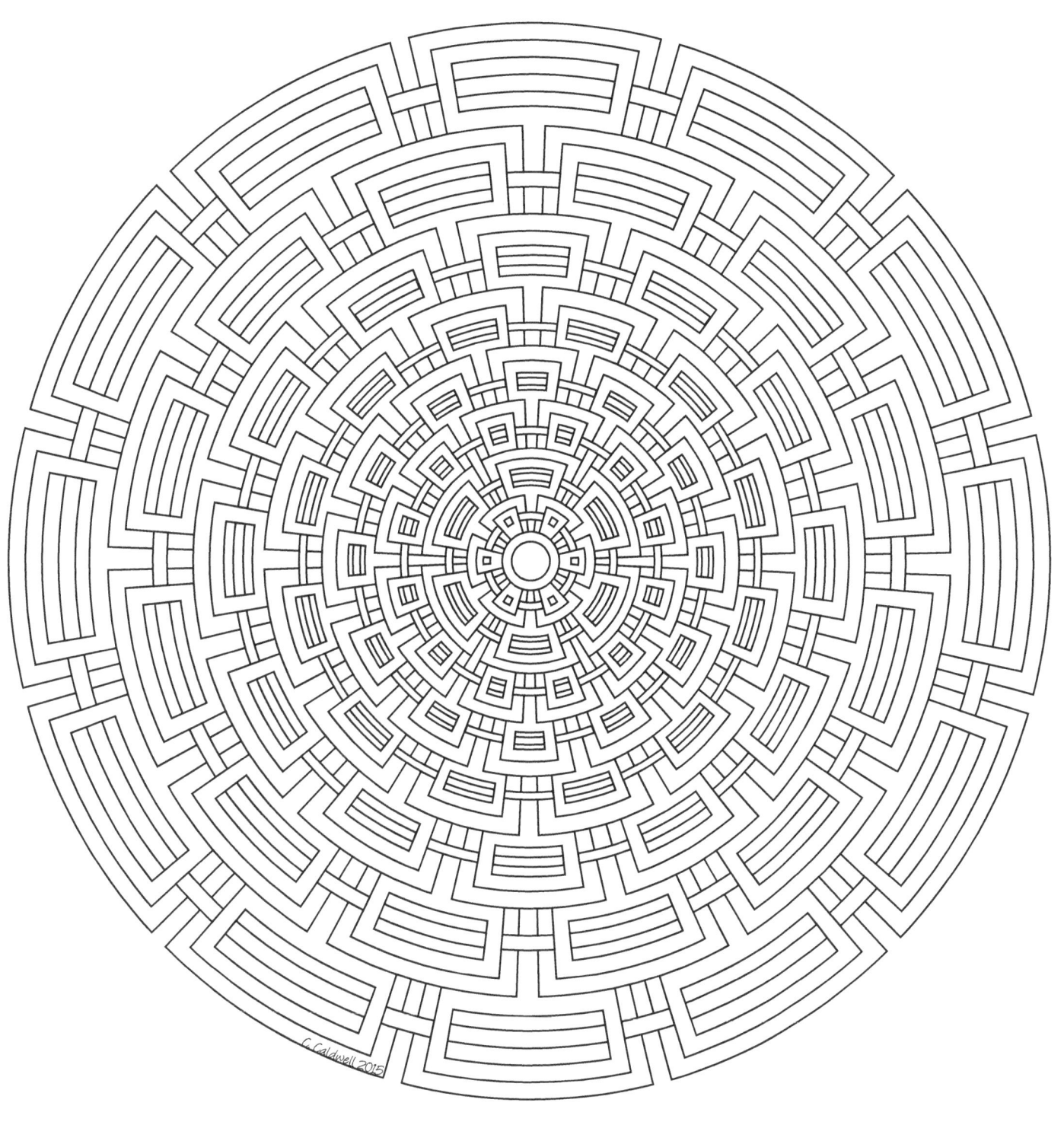

C. Caldwell 2015

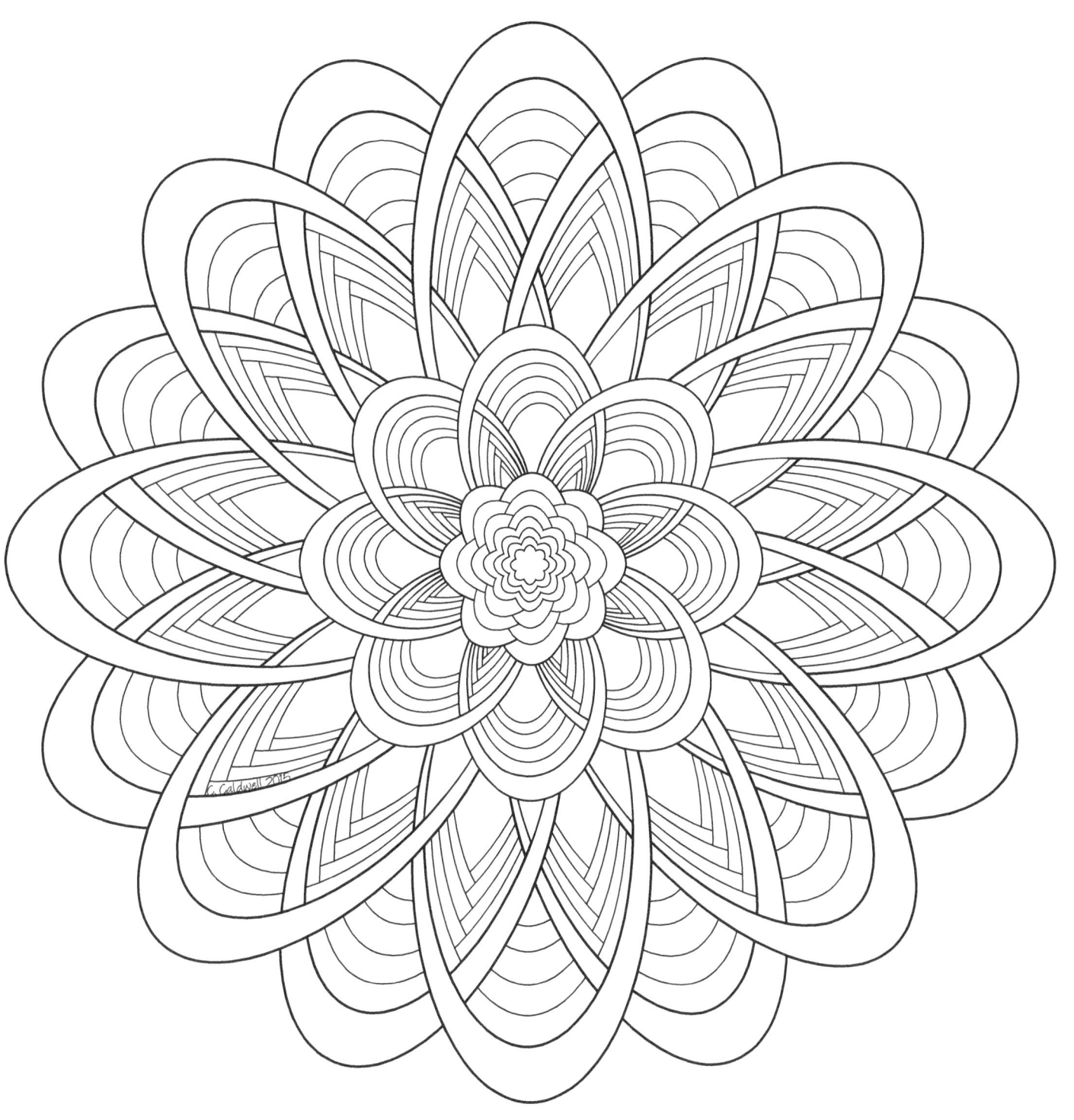

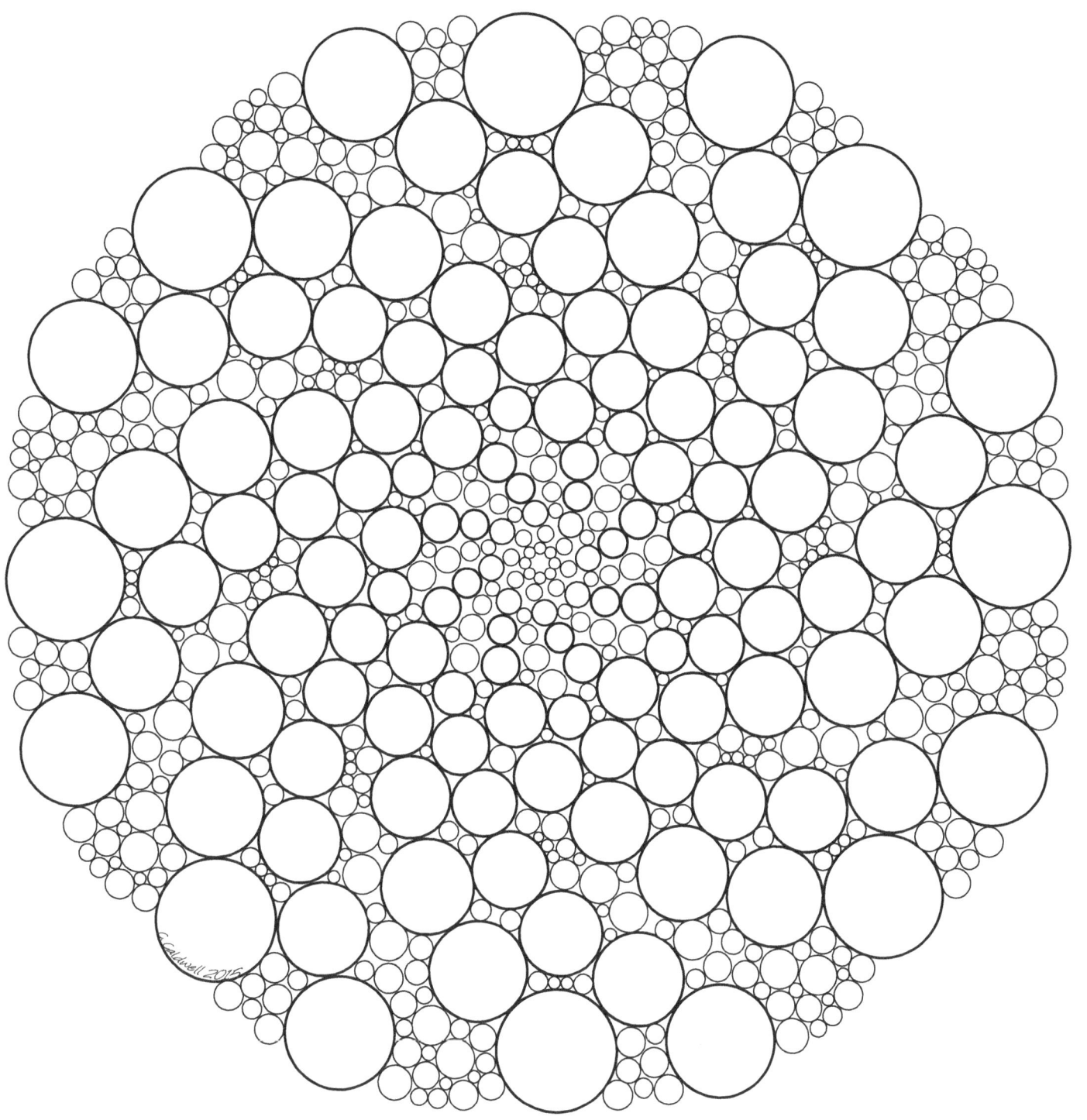

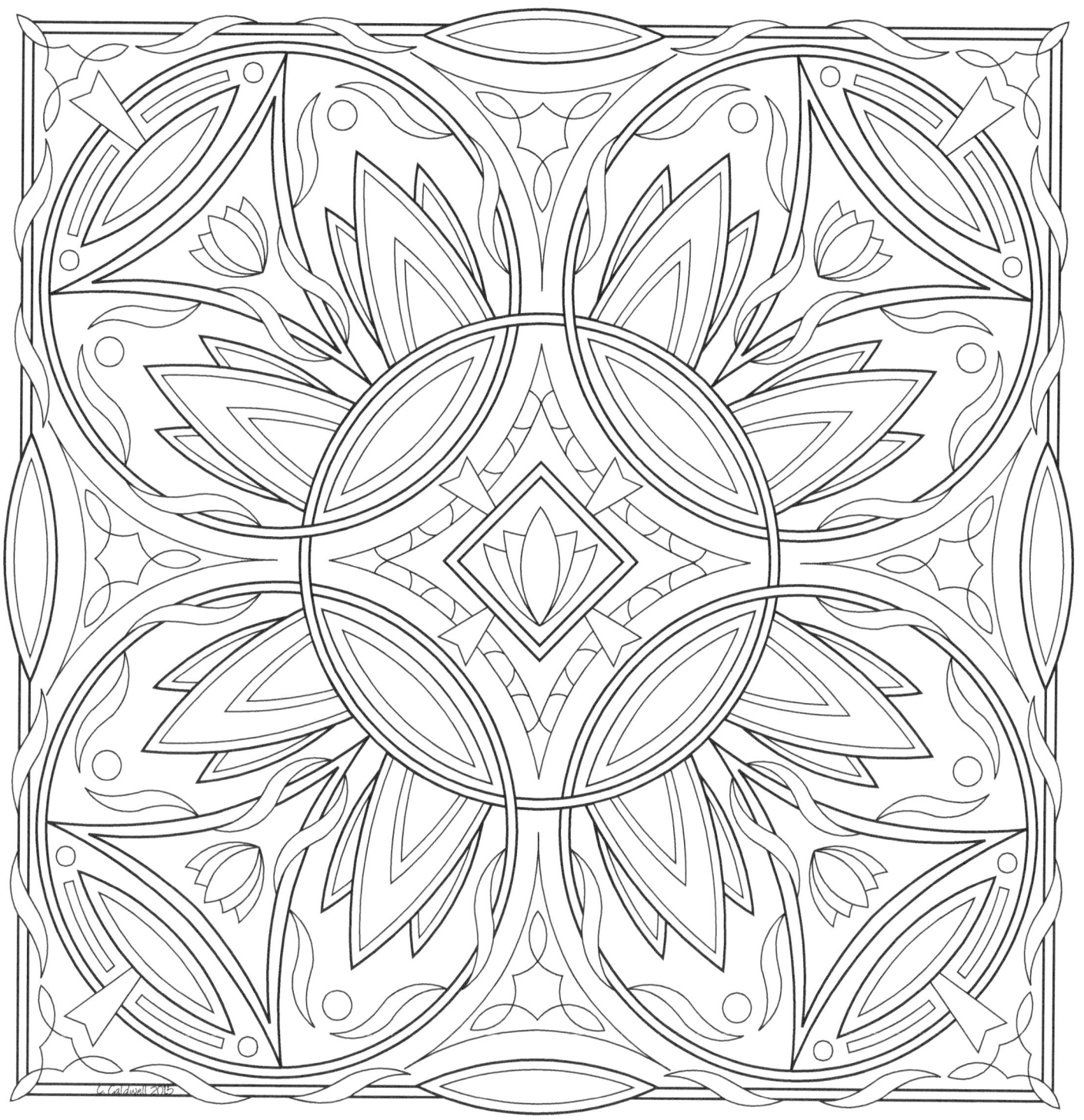

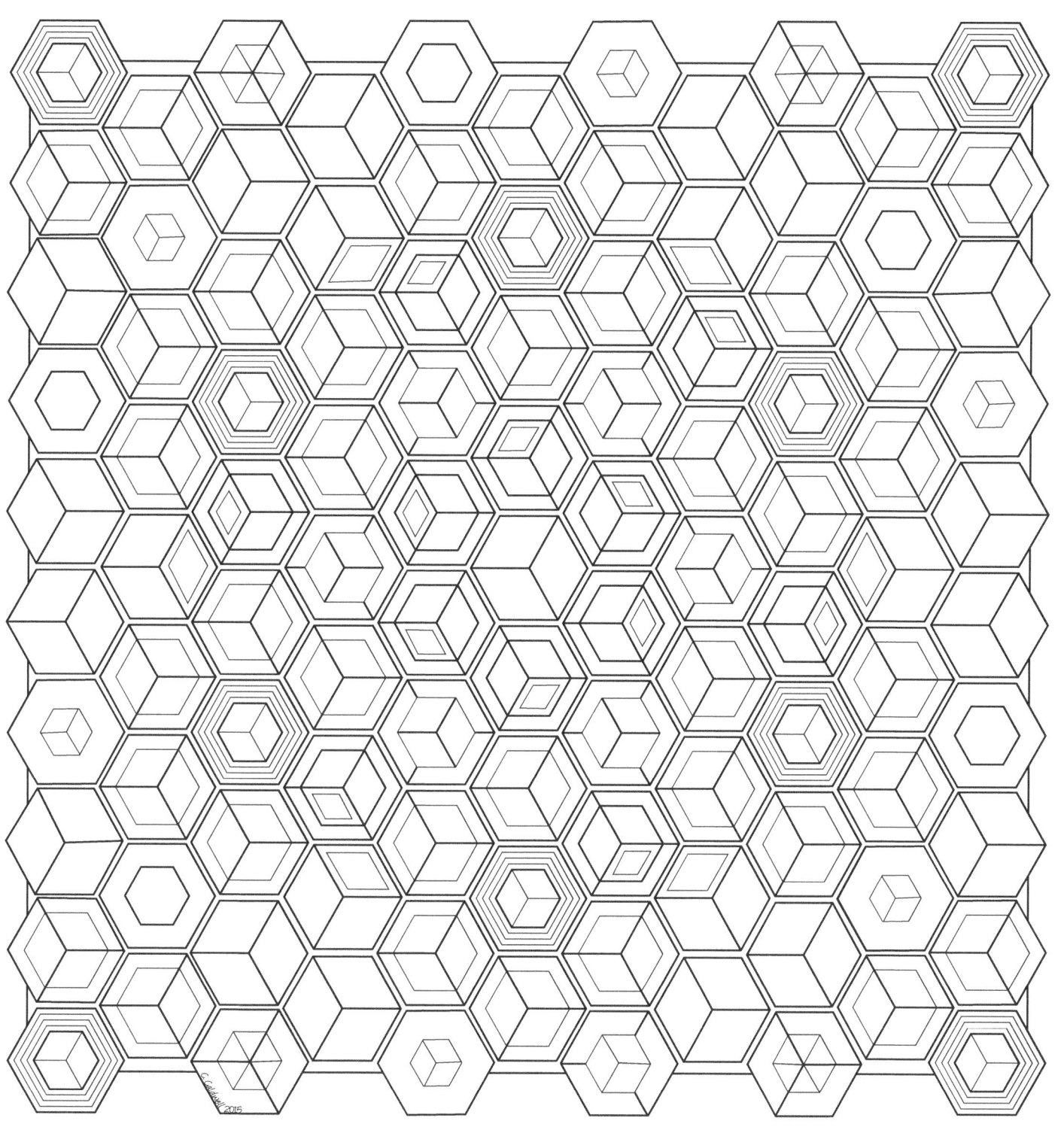

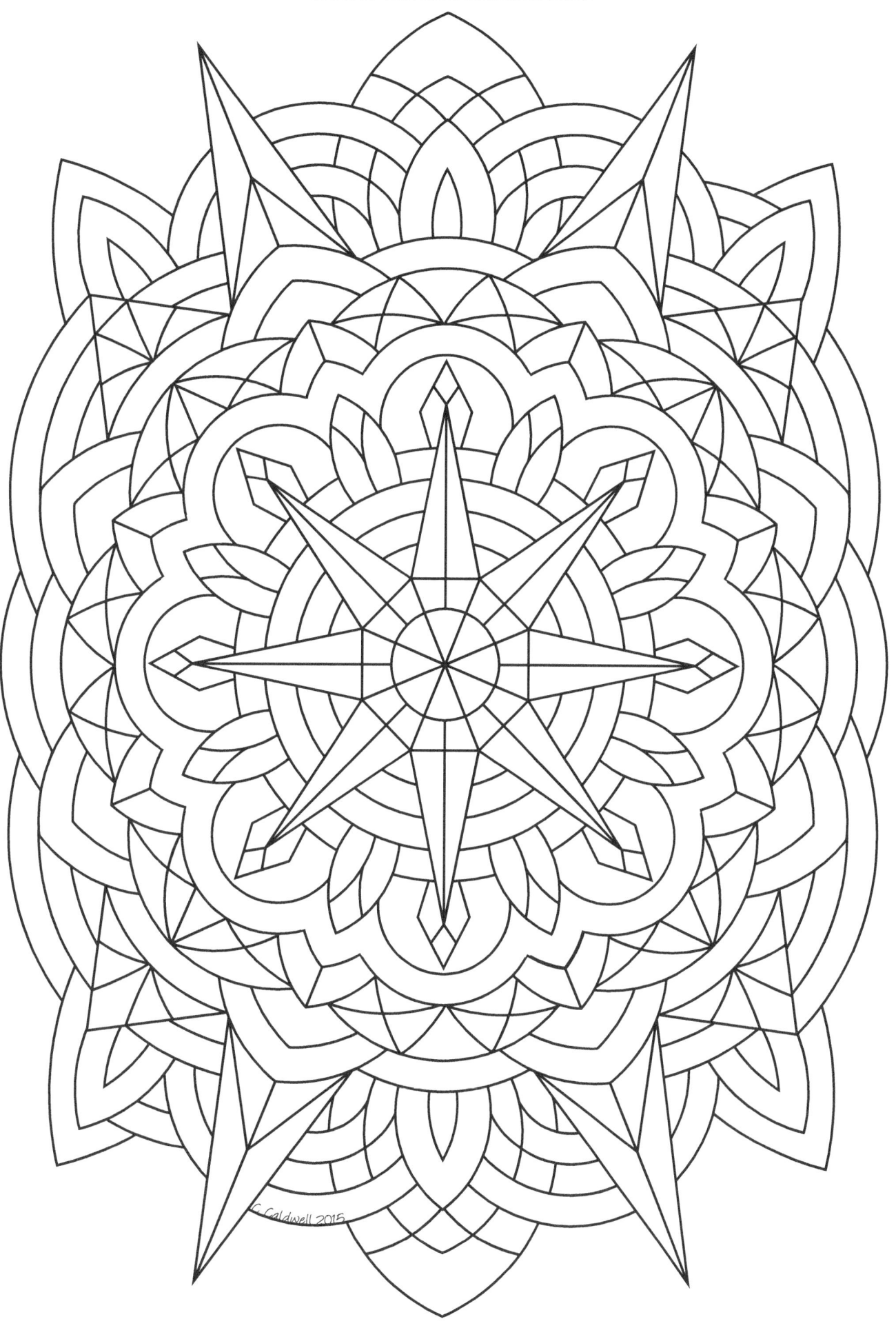

C. Caldwell 2015

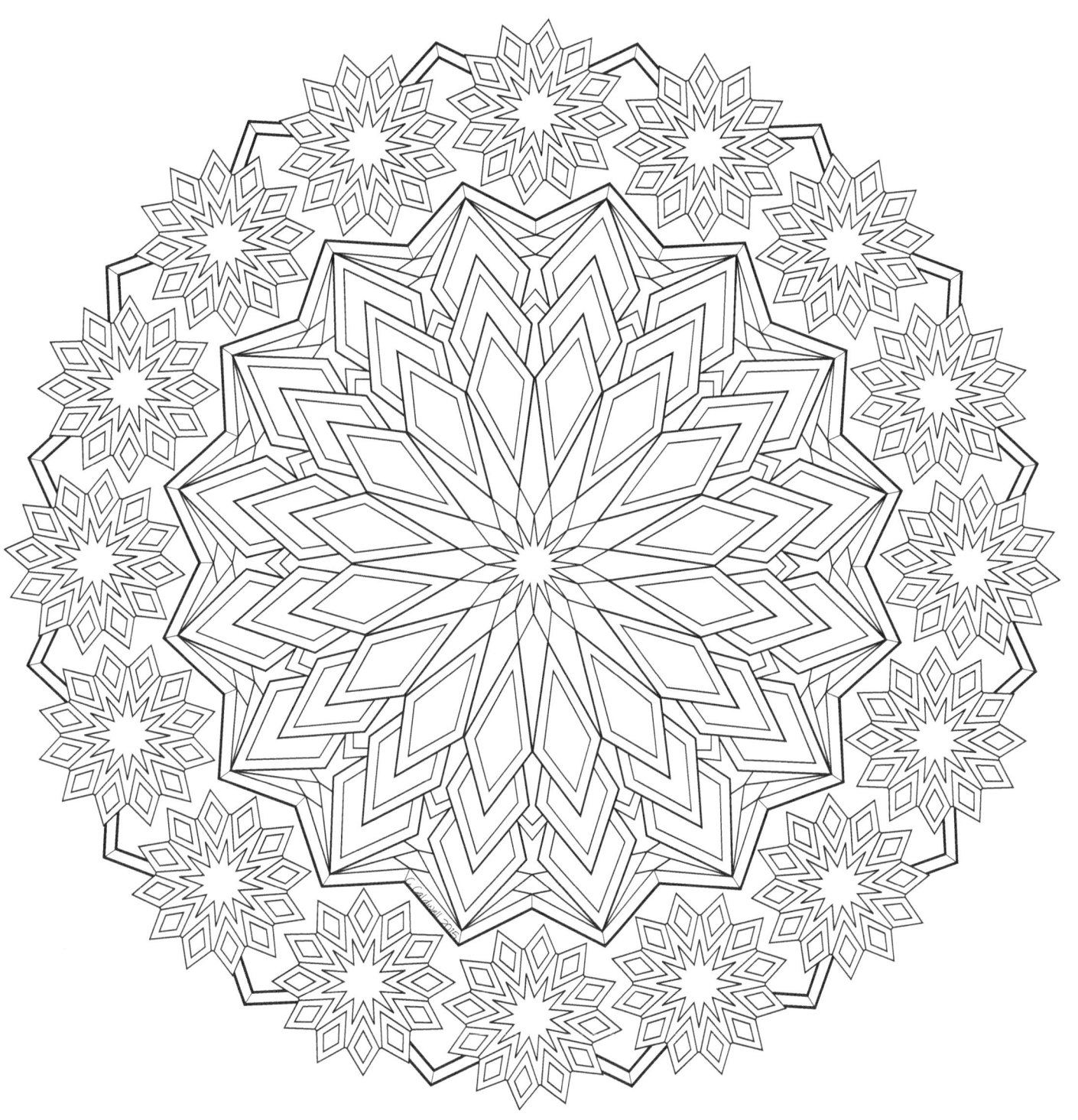

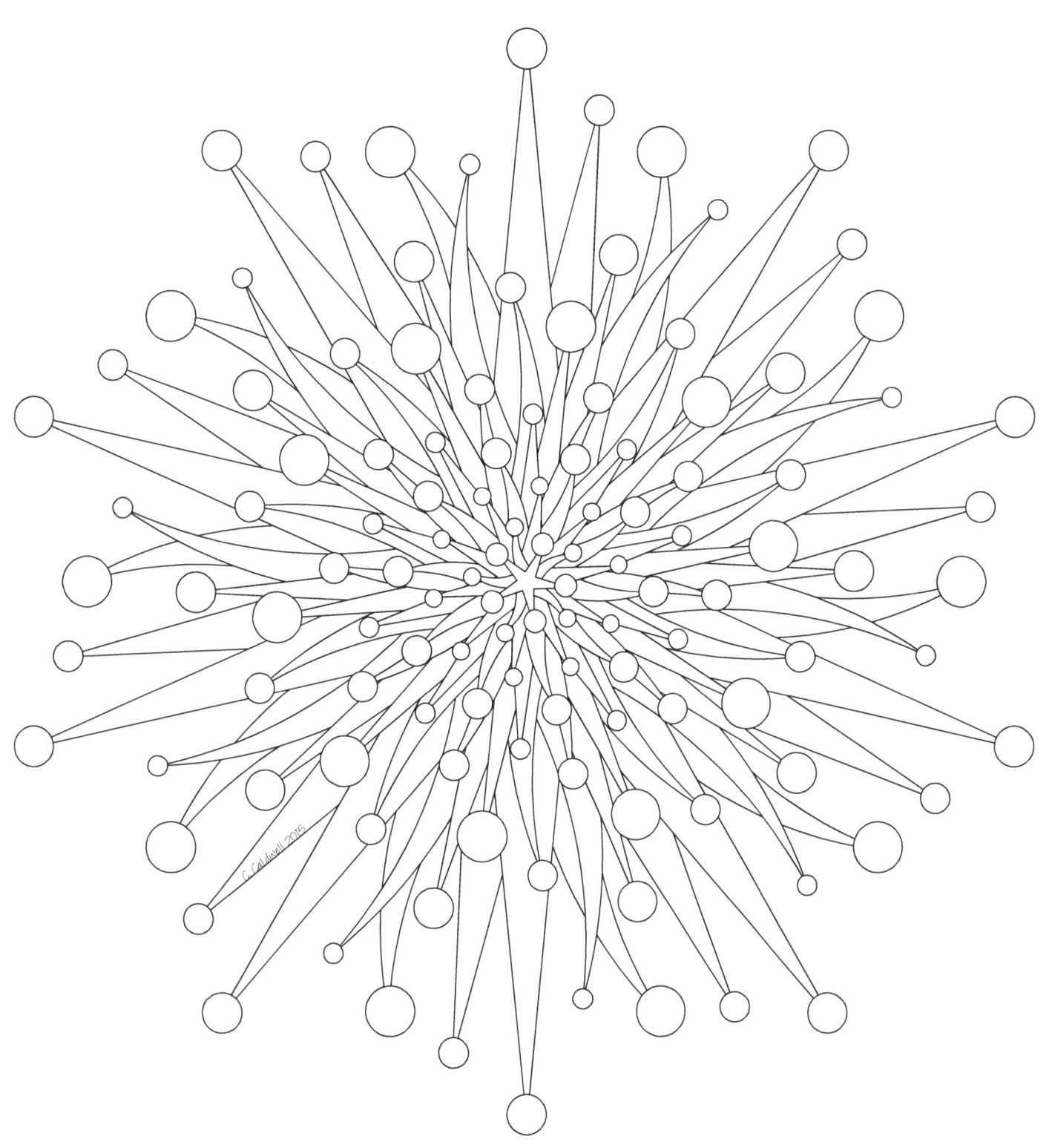

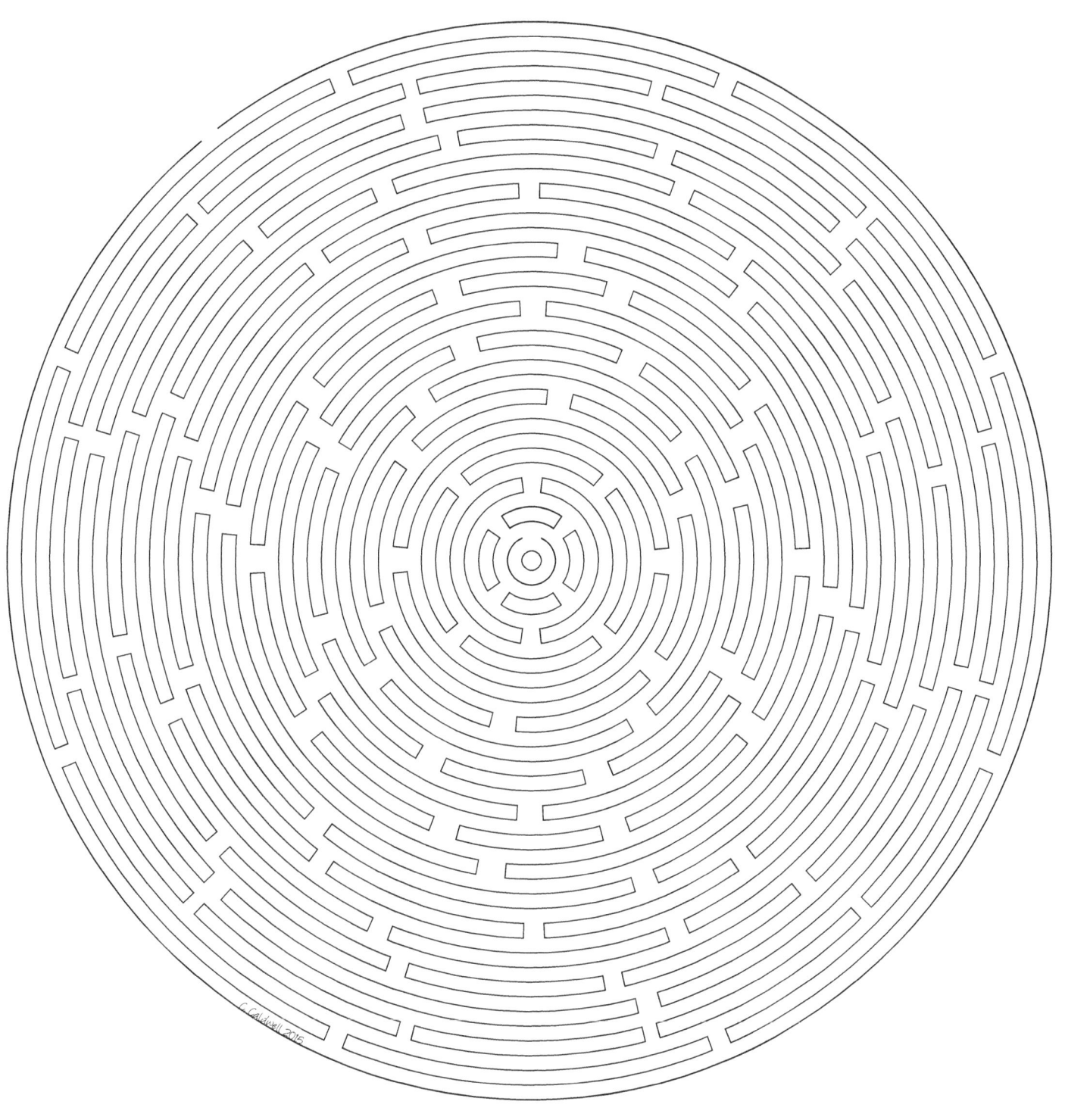

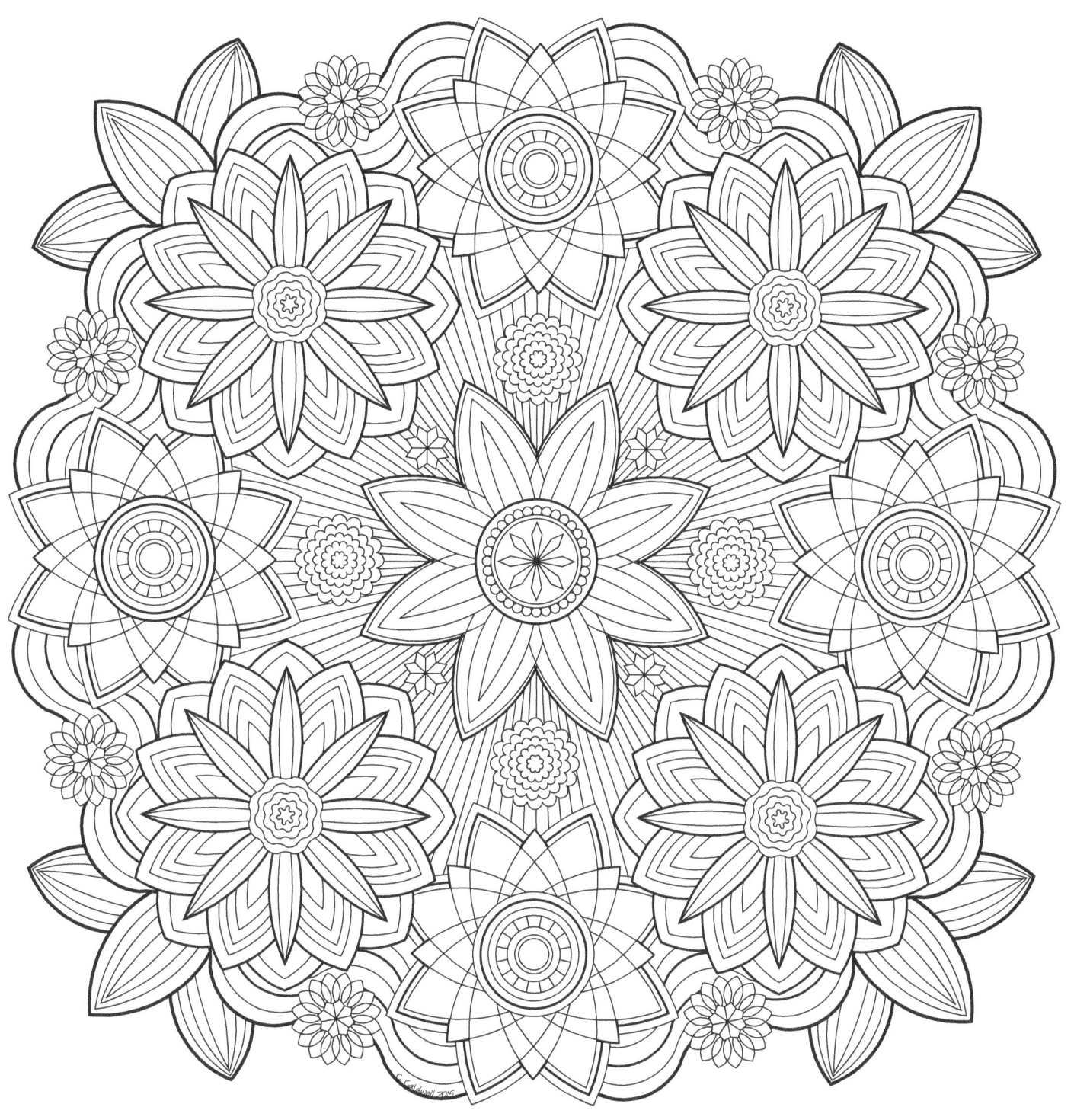

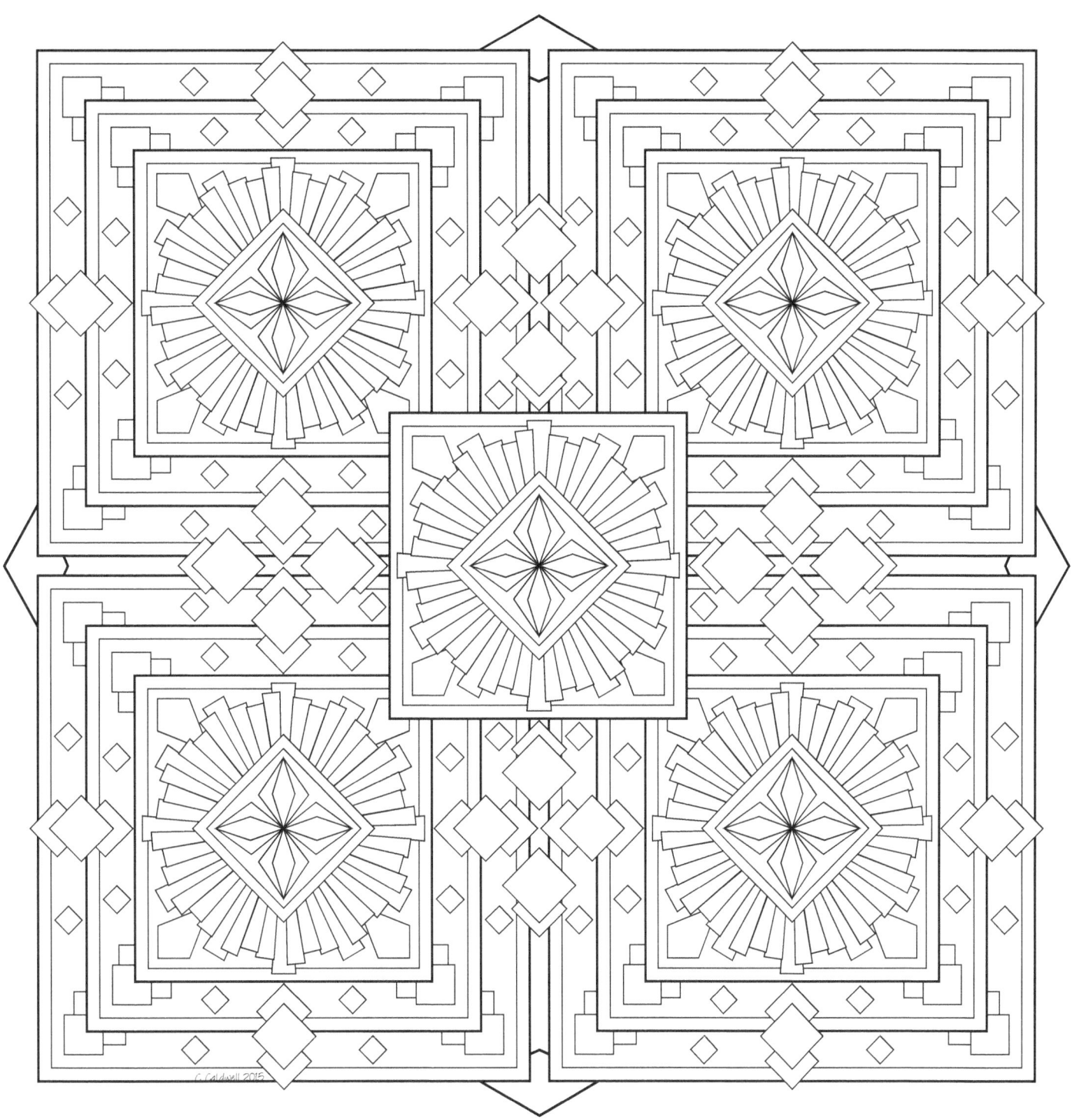

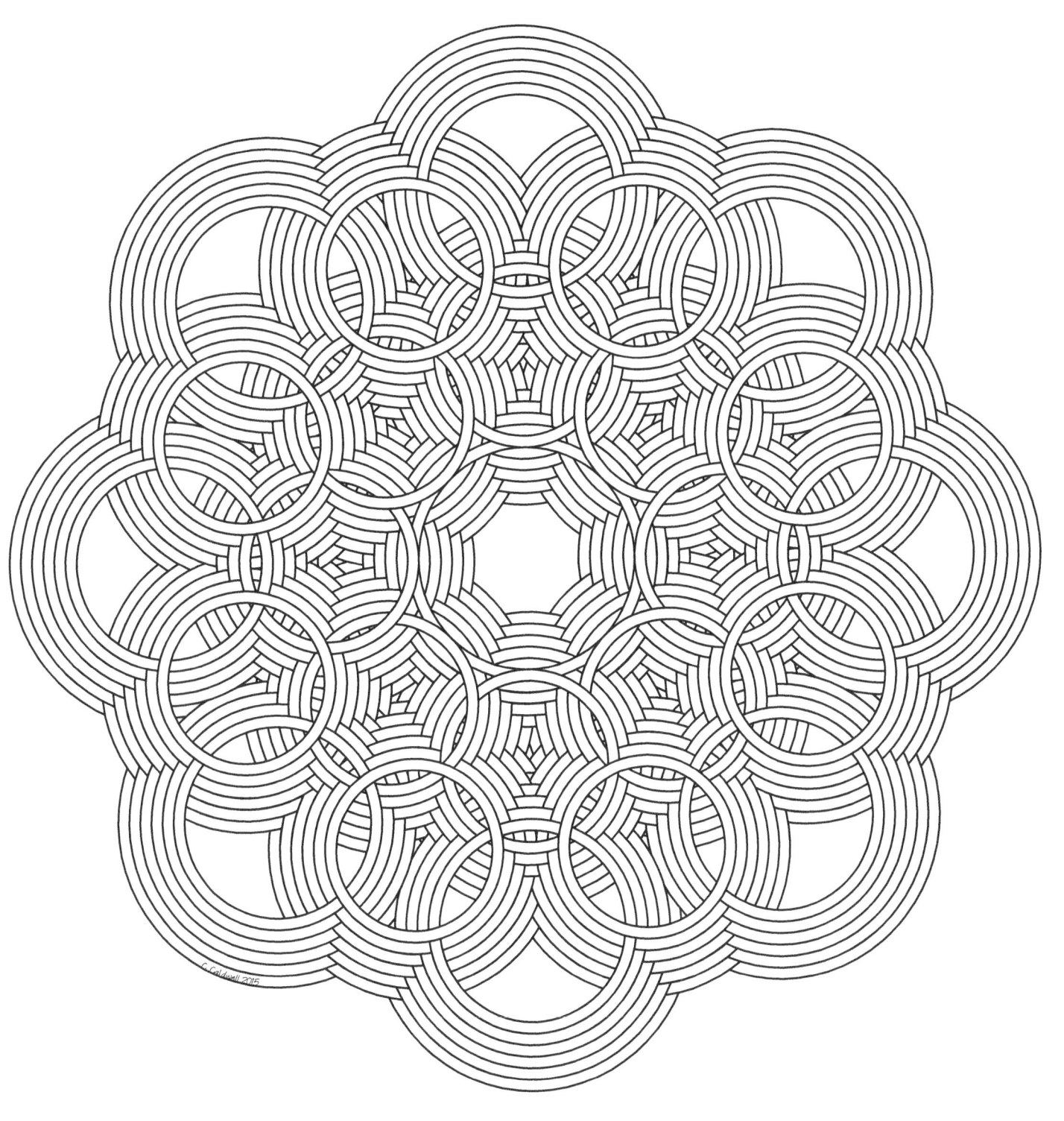

C. Caldwell 2015

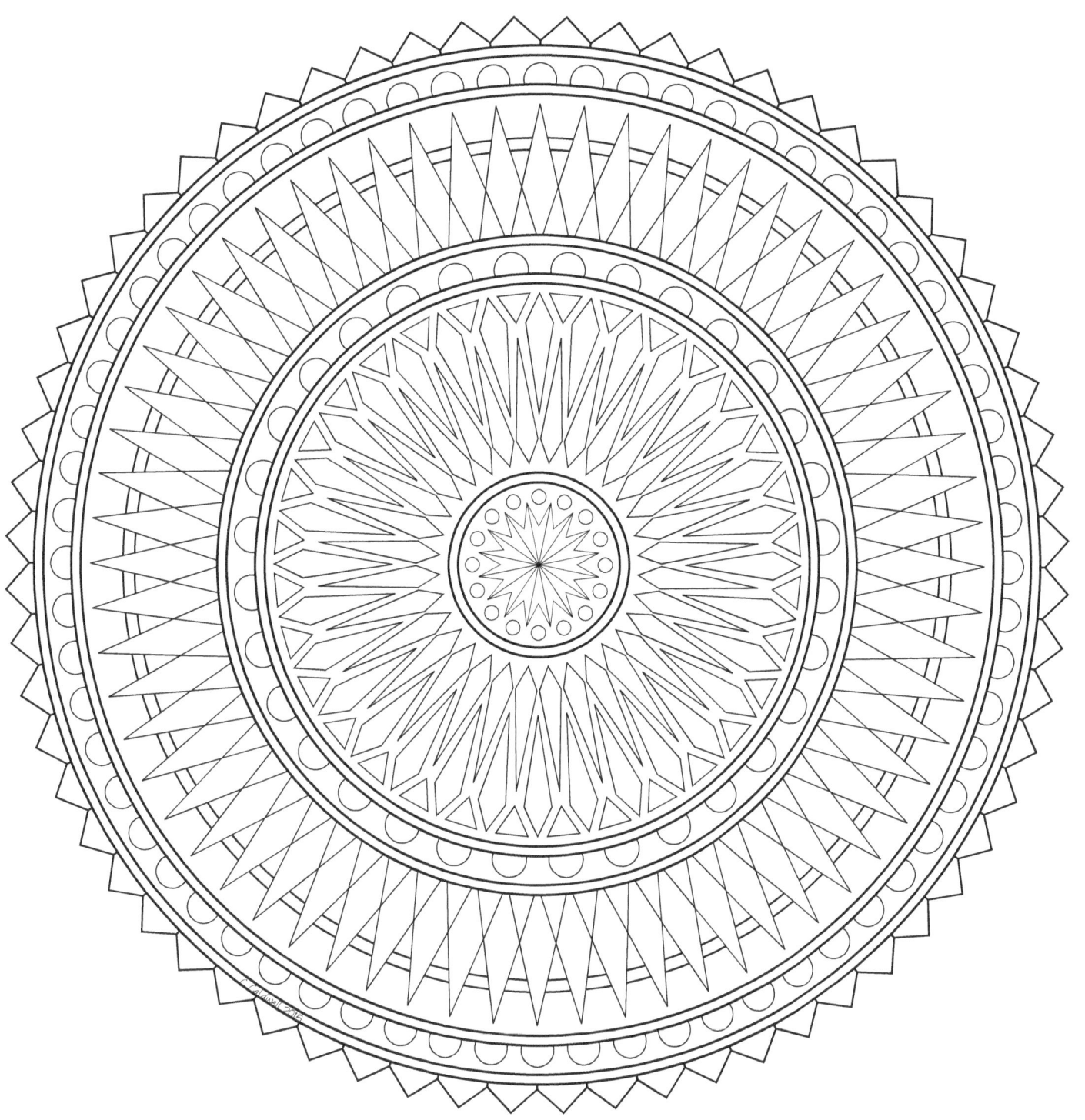

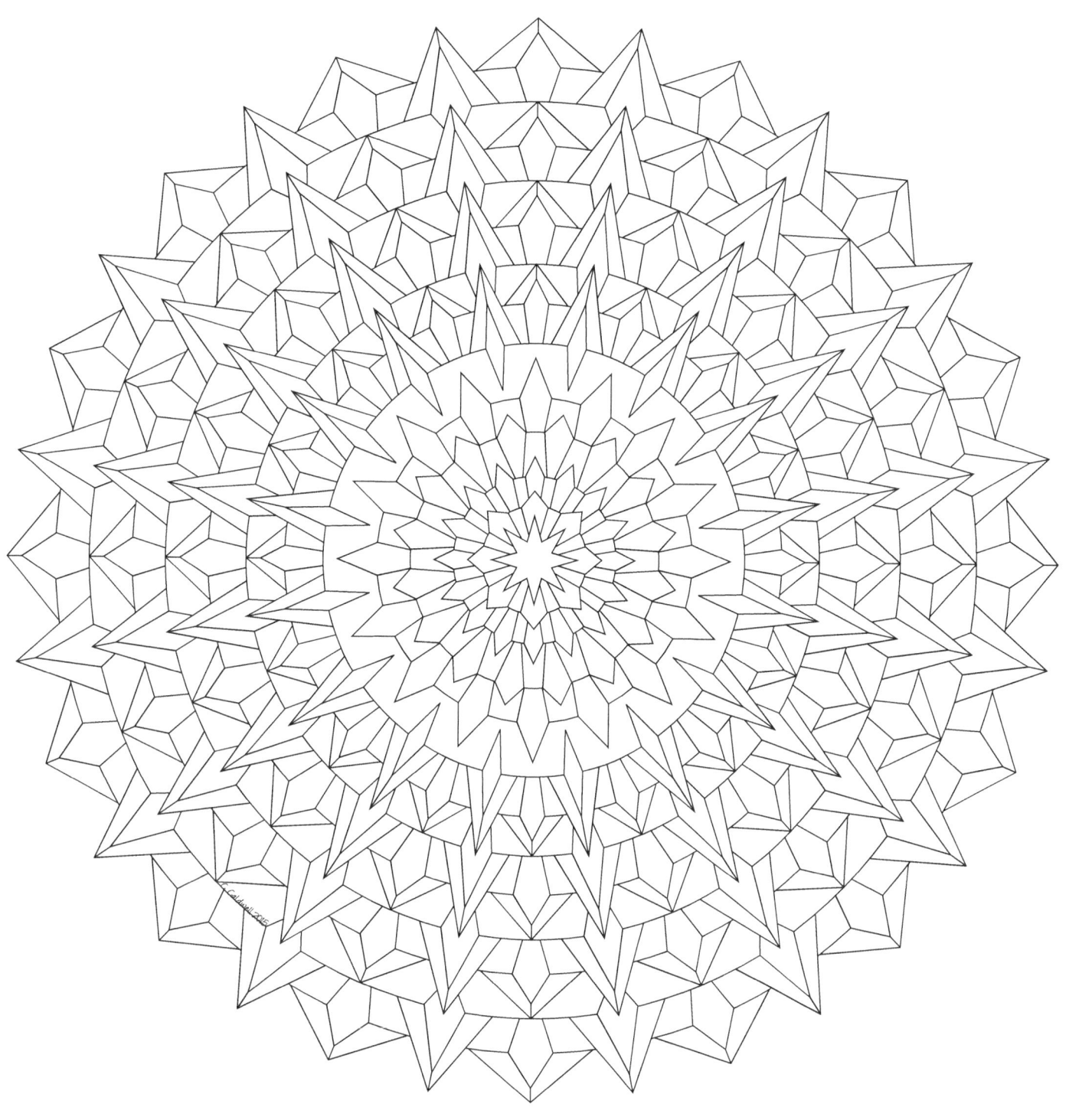

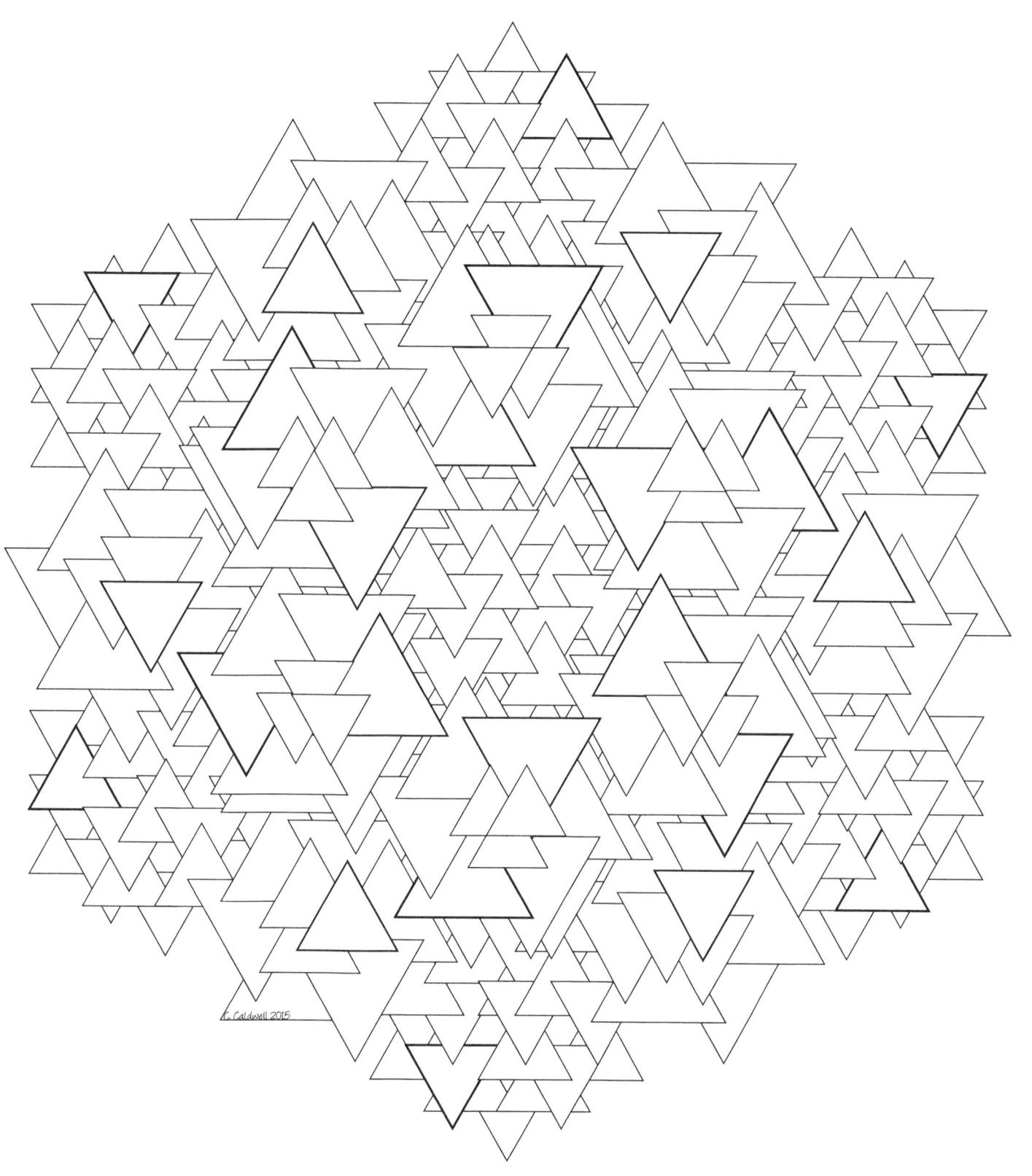

C. Caldwell 2015

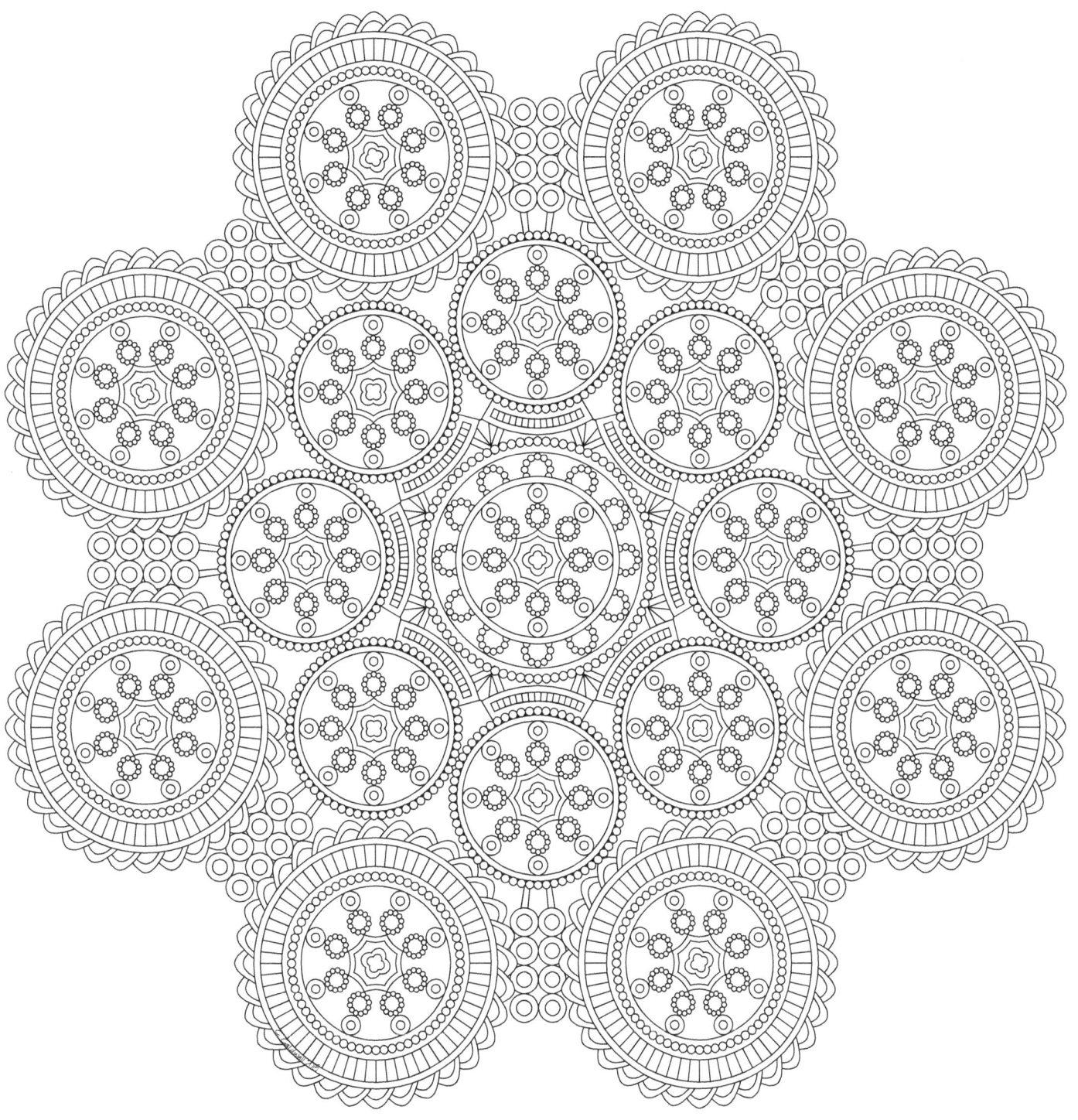

YET ANOTHER MOM COLORING BOOK
SIMPLE SYMMETRY, VOLUME 1
MANDALAS & MORE

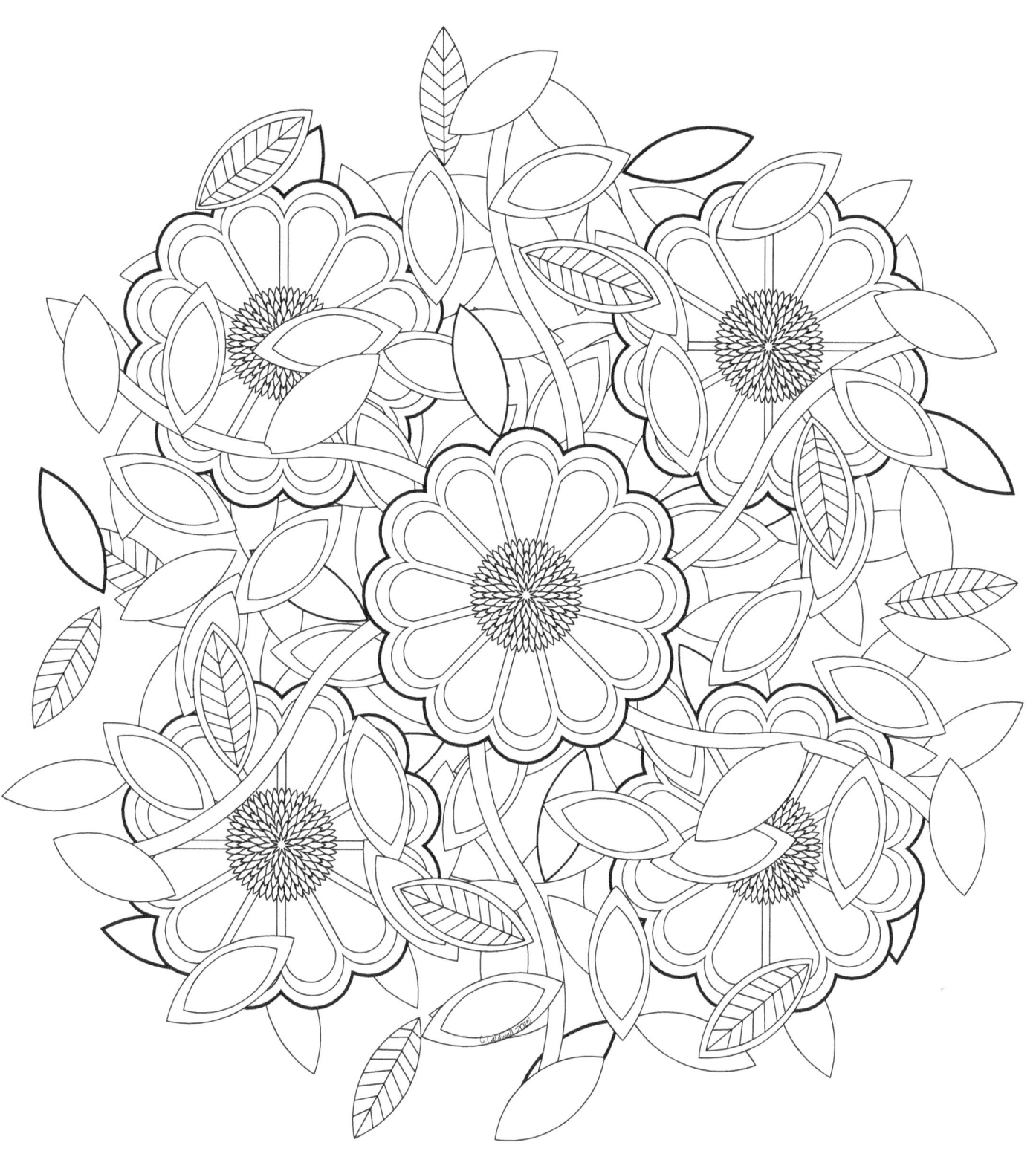

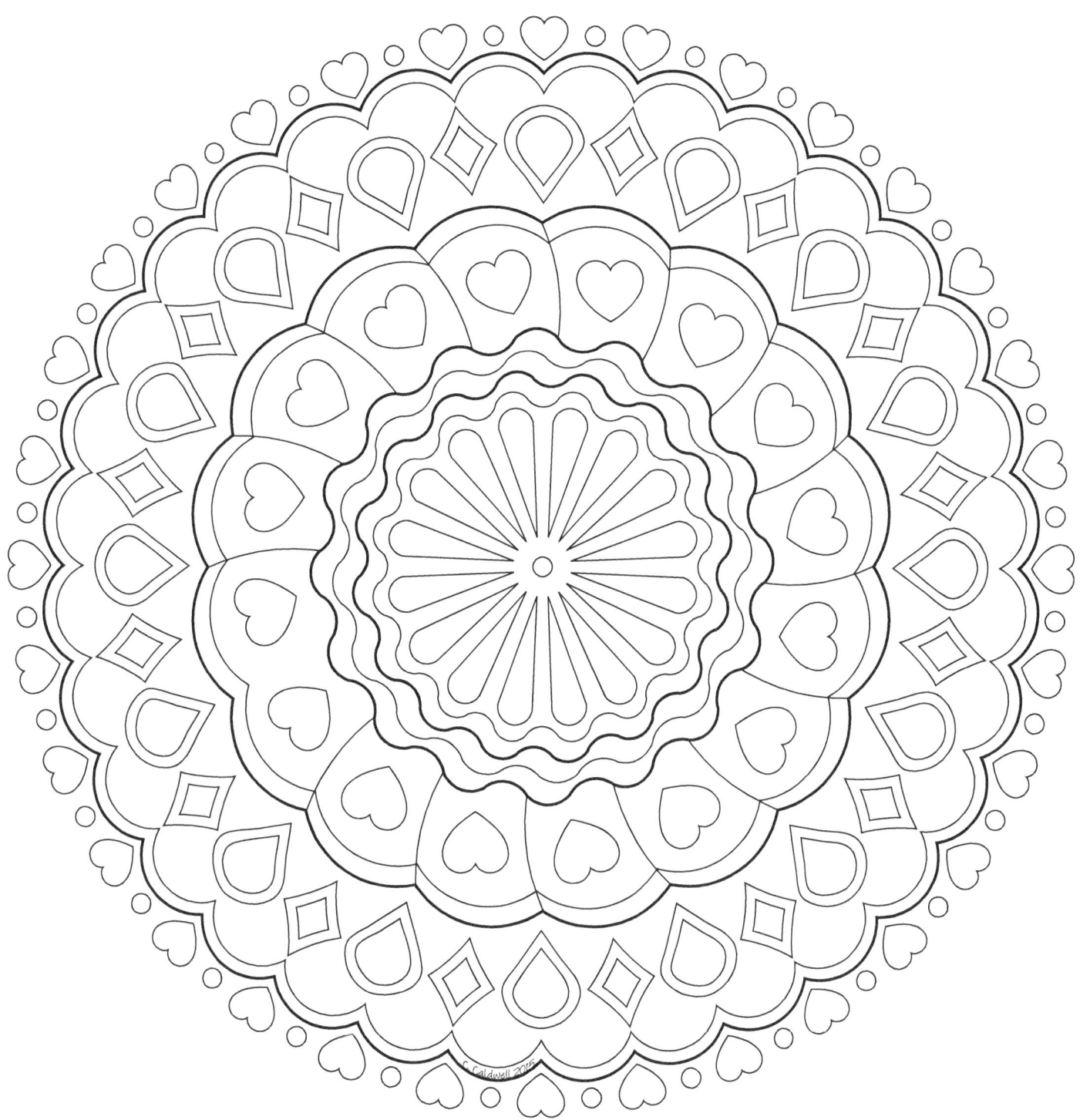

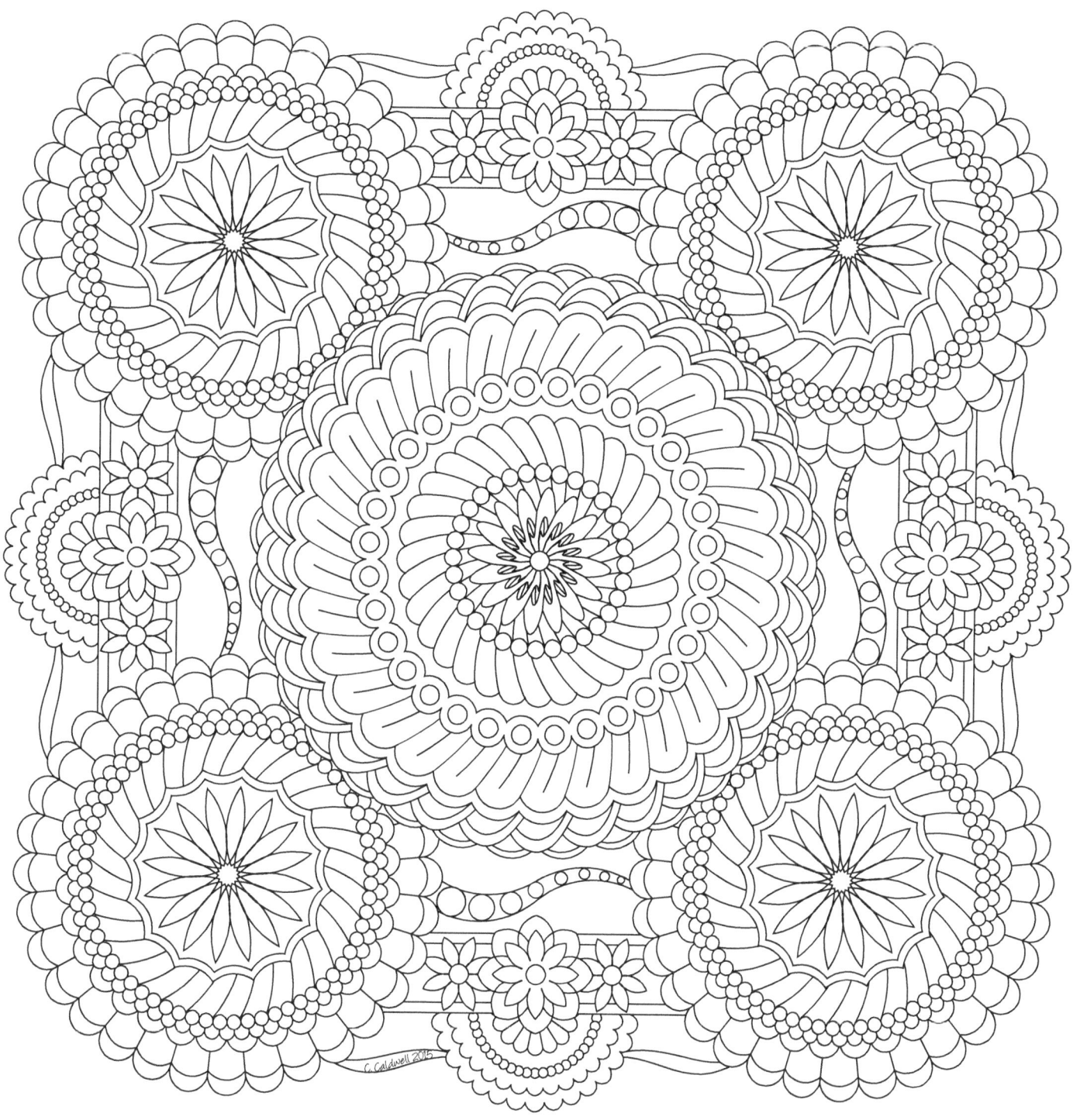

C. Caldwell 2015

The design on the facing page was done by my six-year-old daughter. She loves copying what Mommy does, and this includes creating coloring pages. She has drawn many abstract coloring pages, but this was her first attempt at creating a mandala on the computer. I think she did an excellent job! I told her I would publish it if I ever created a coloring book, so here it is!

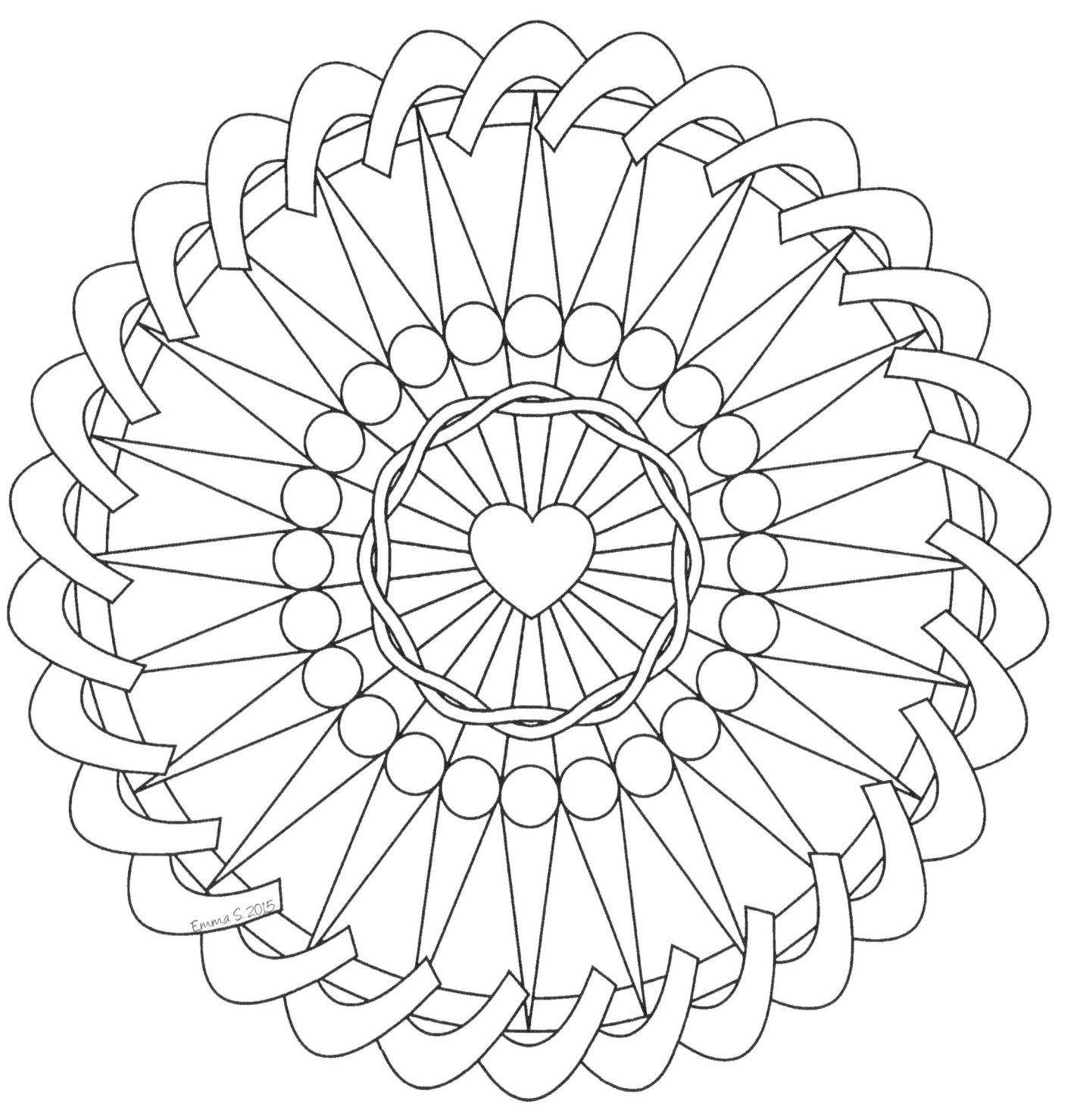

YET ANOTHER MOM COLORING BOOK
SIMPLE SYMMETRY, VOLUME 1
MANDALAS & MORE

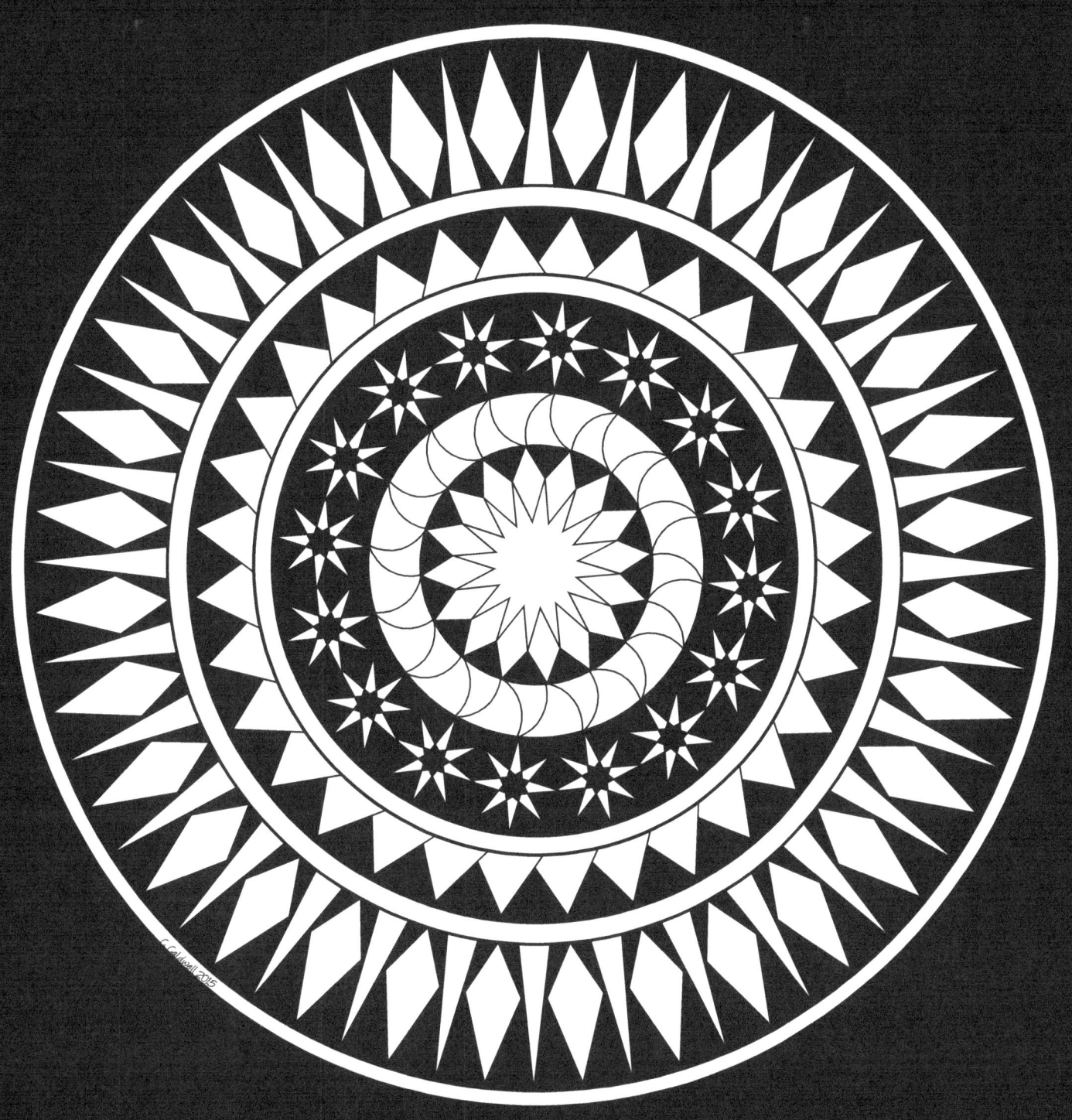

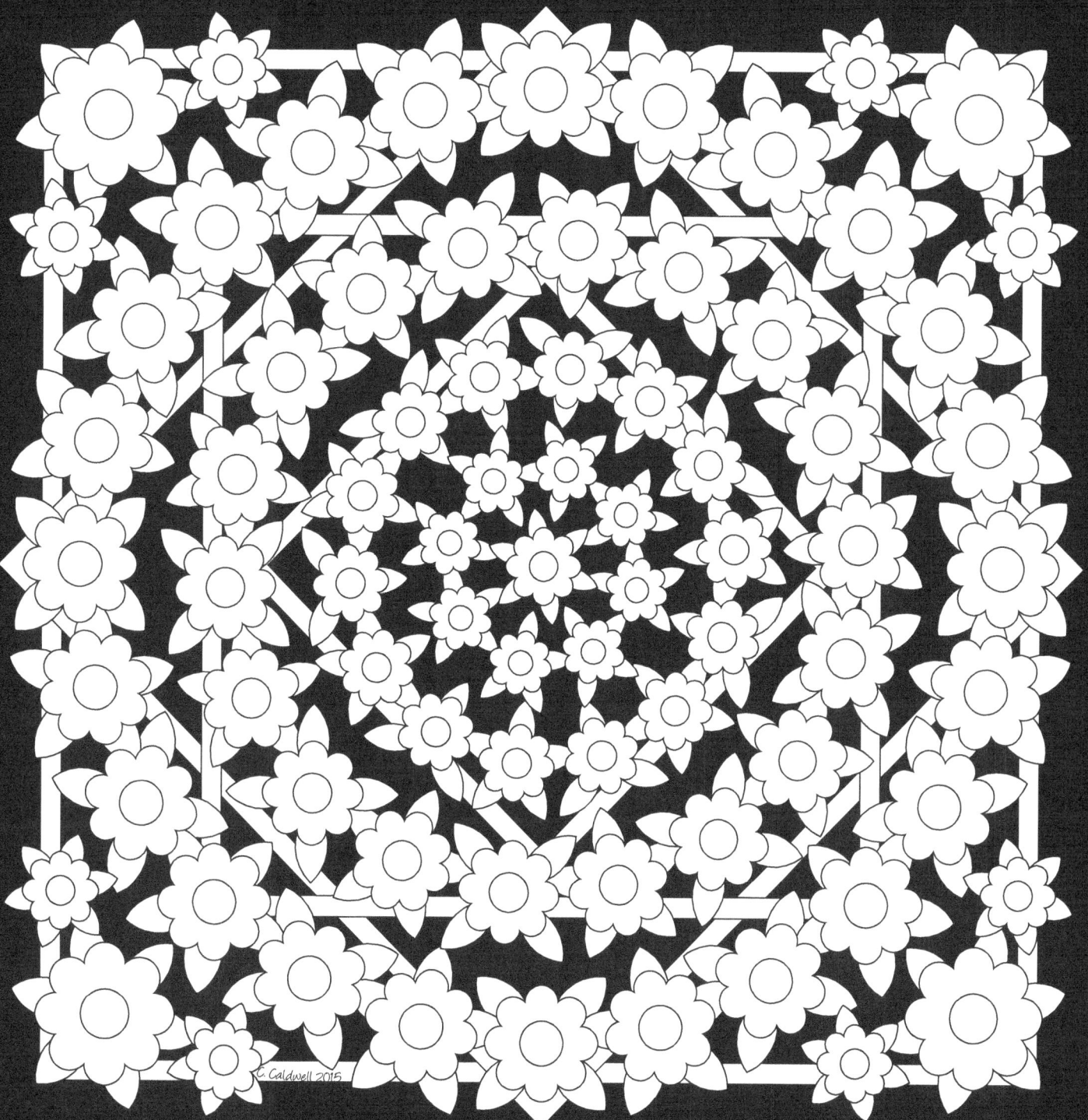

C. Caldwell 2015

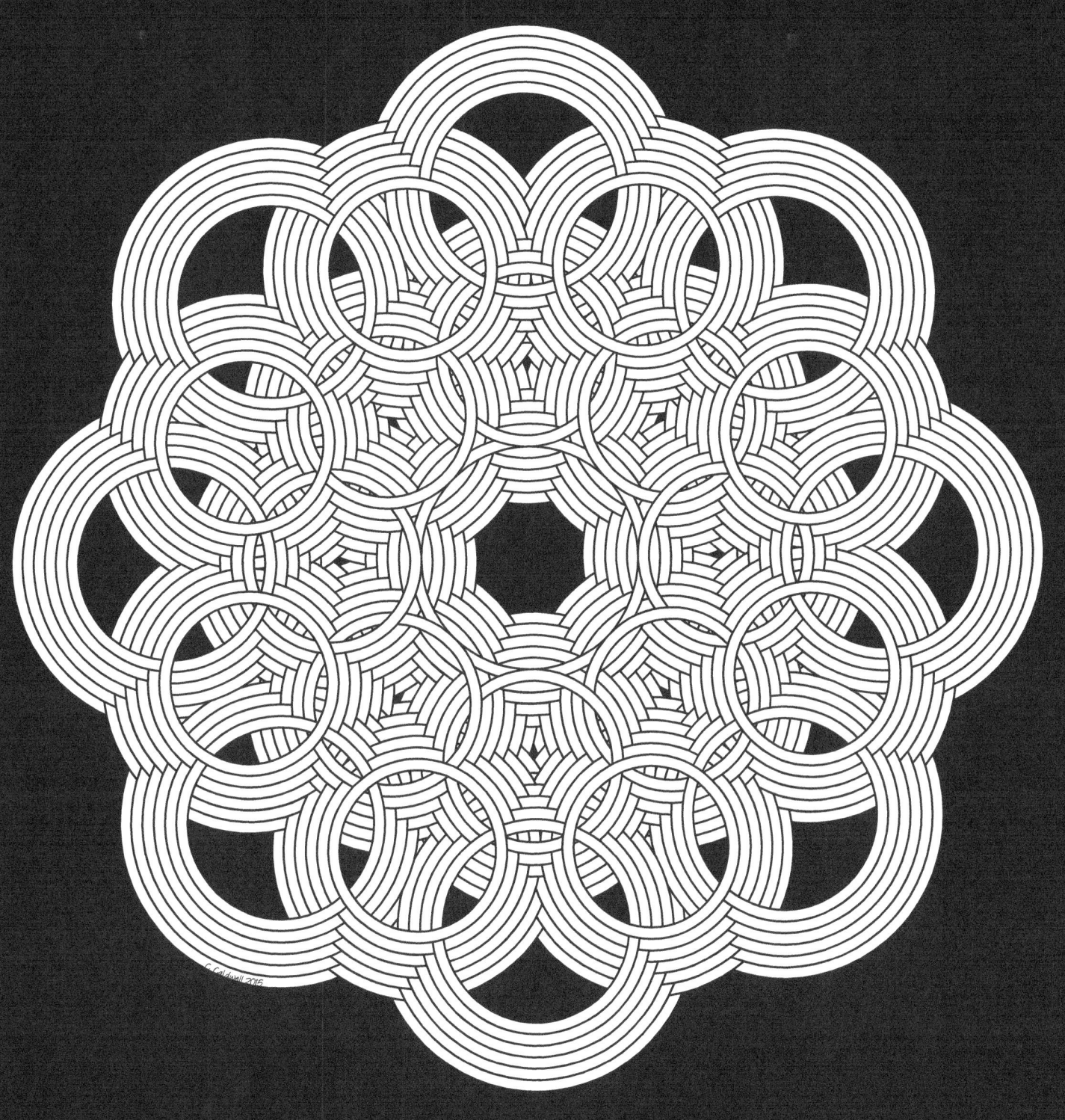

YET ANOTHER MOM COLORING BOOK
SIMPLE SYMMETRY, VOLUME 1
MANDALAS & MORE

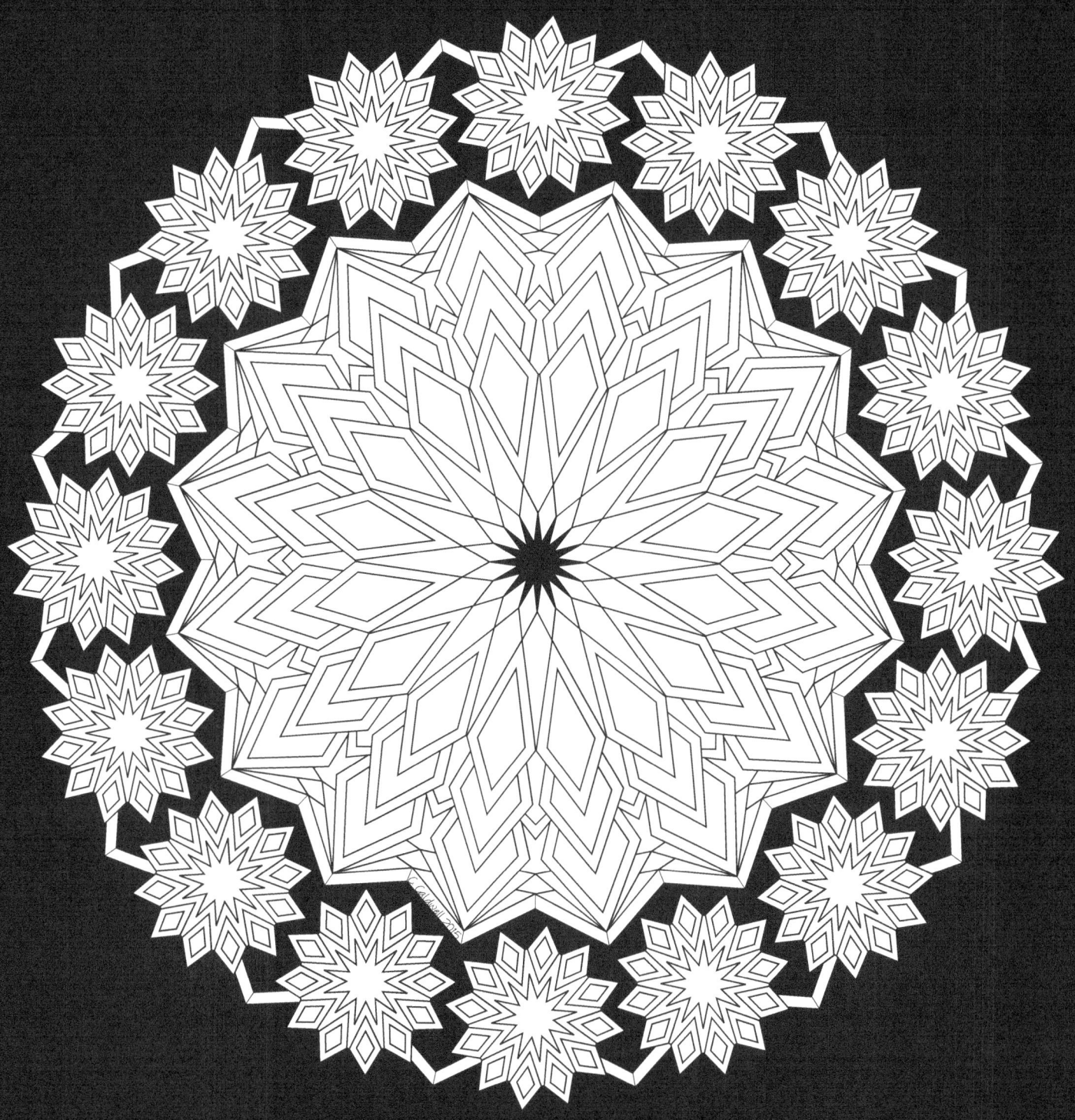

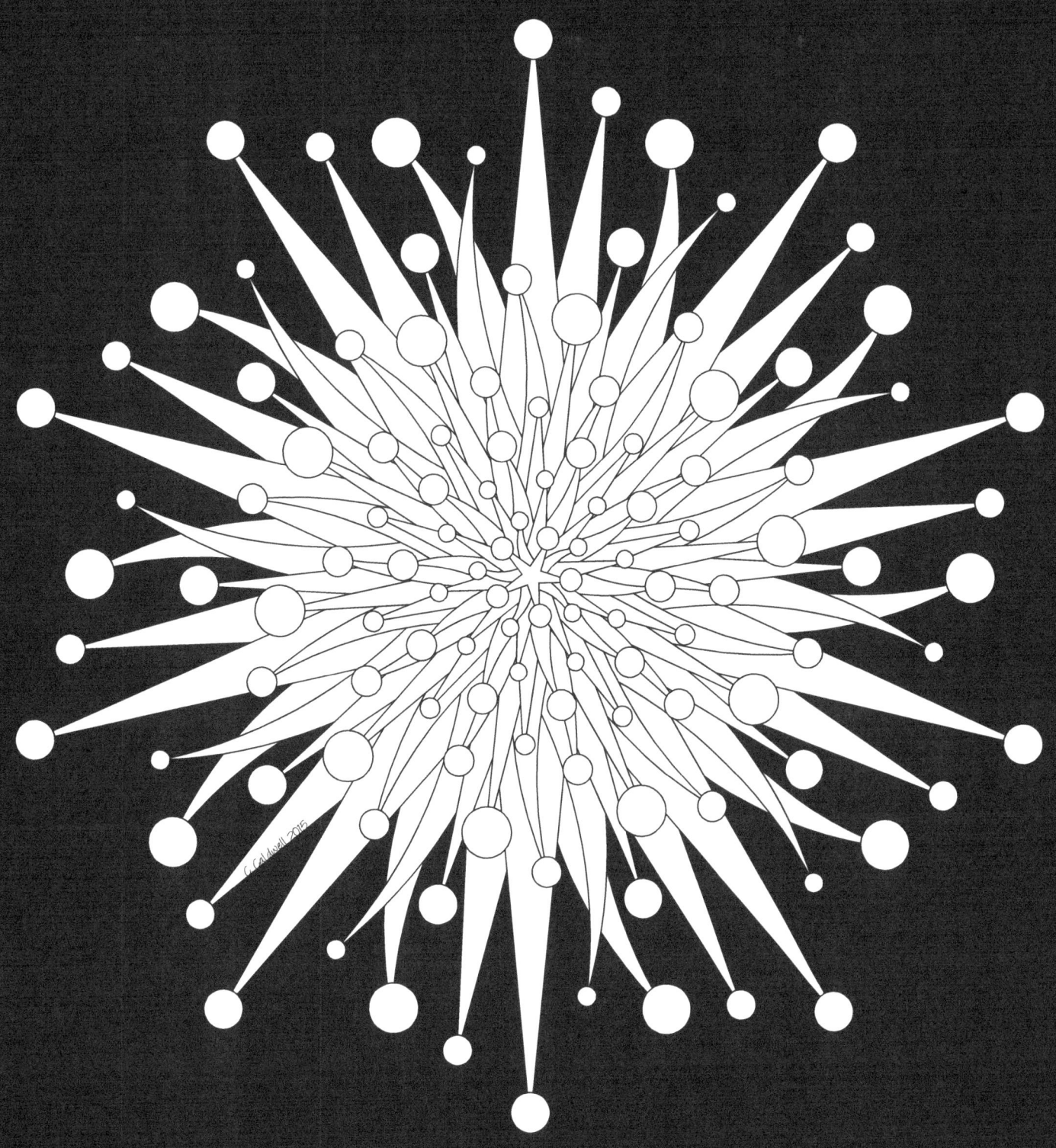

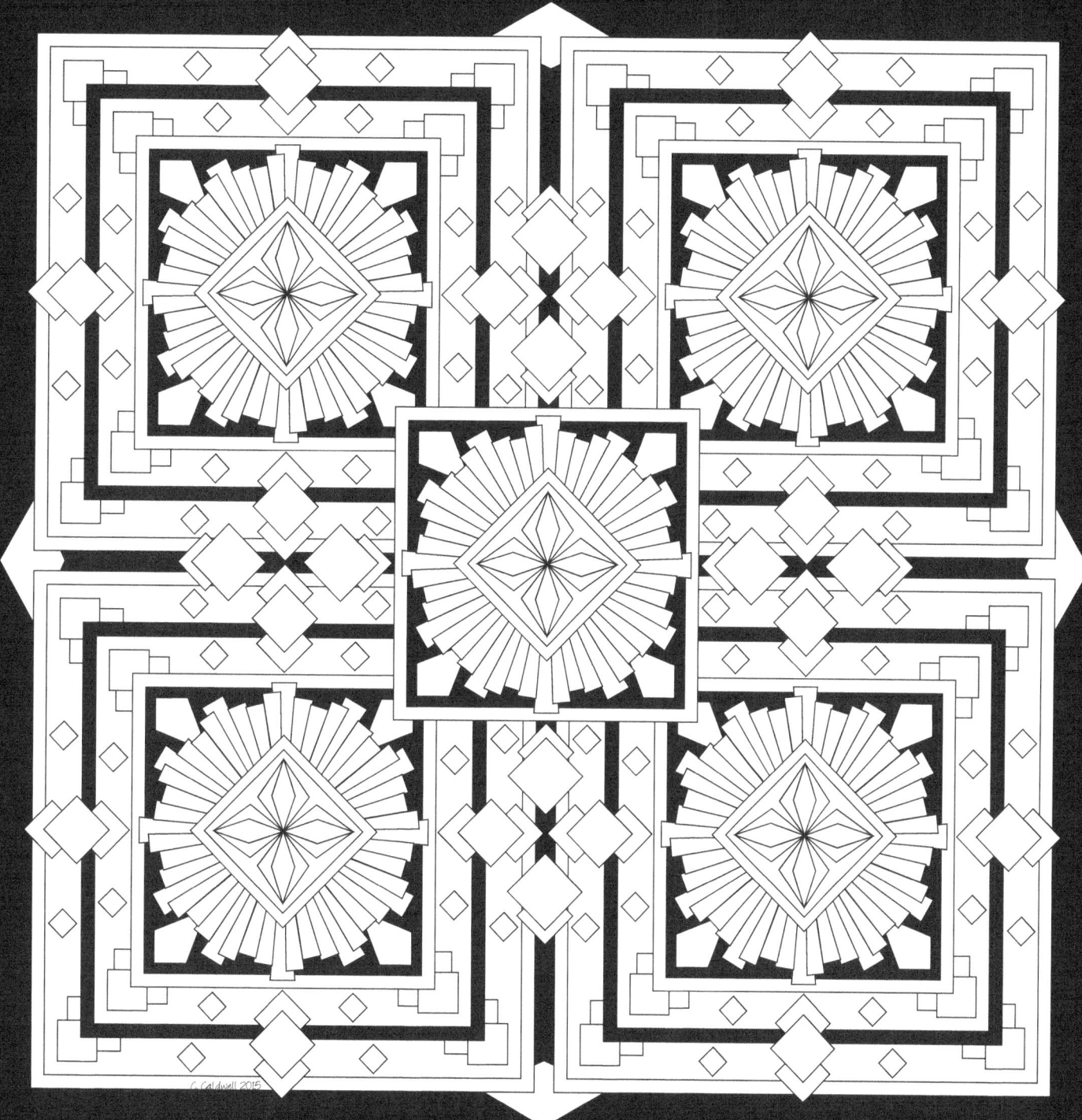

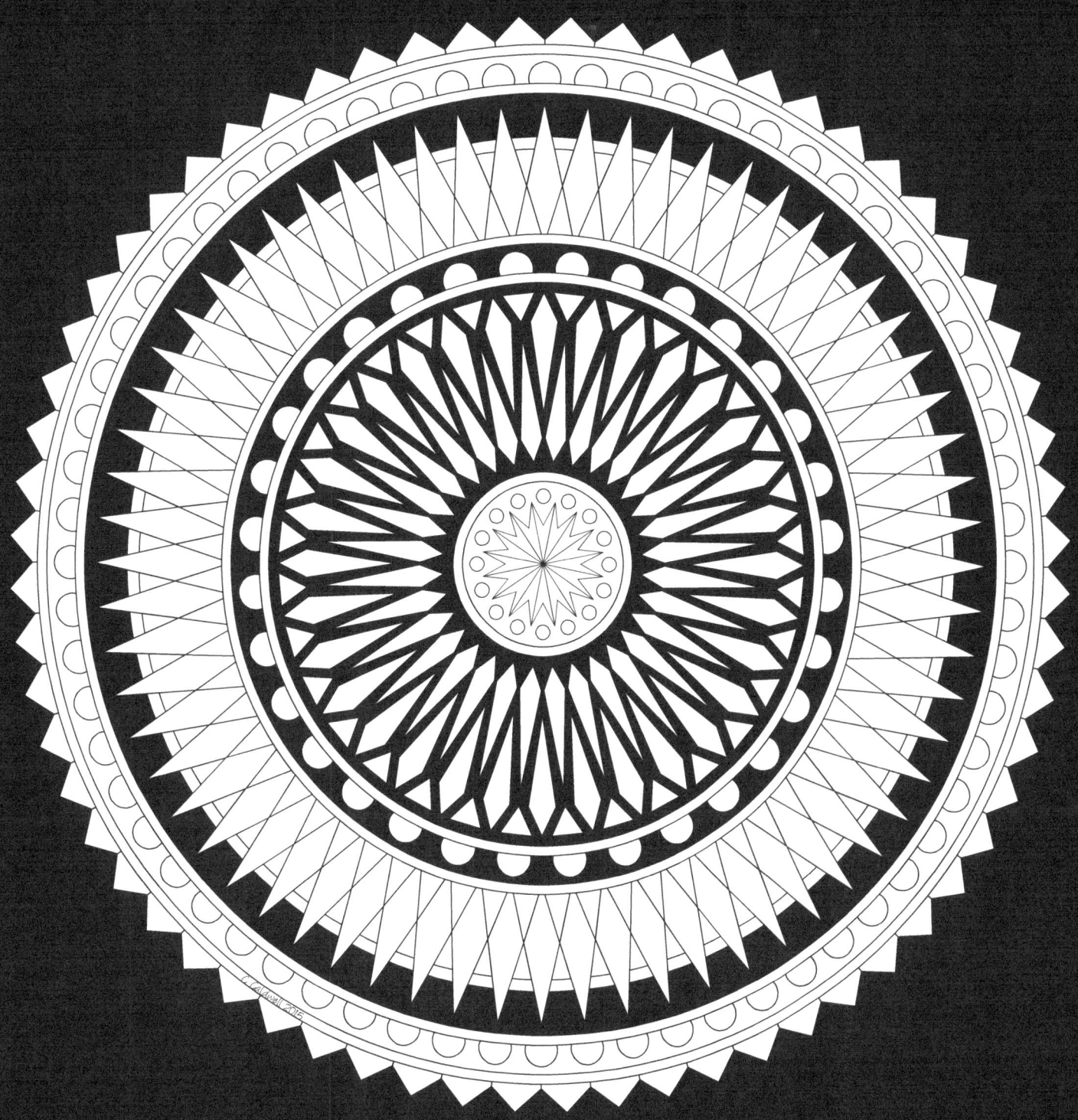

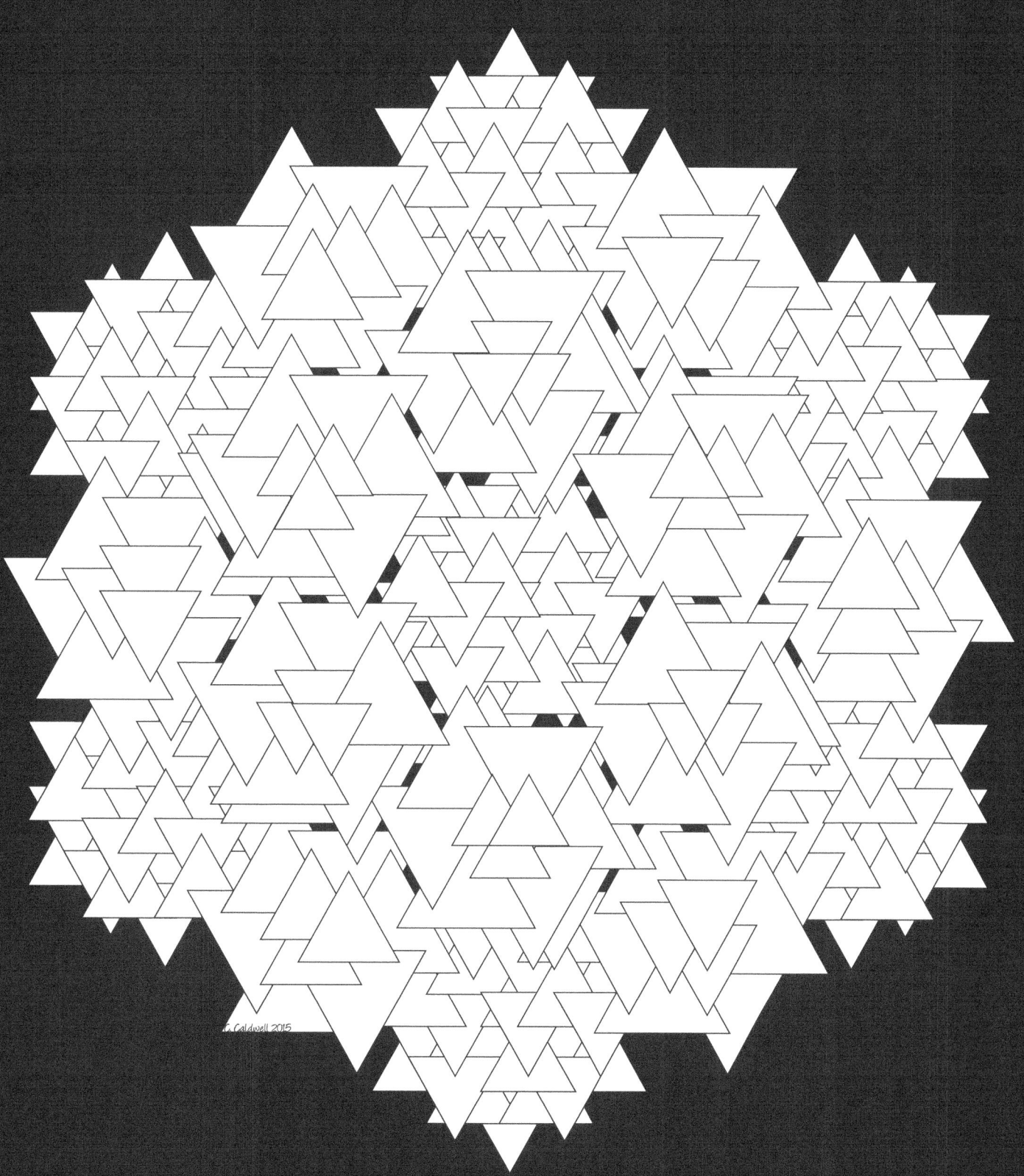

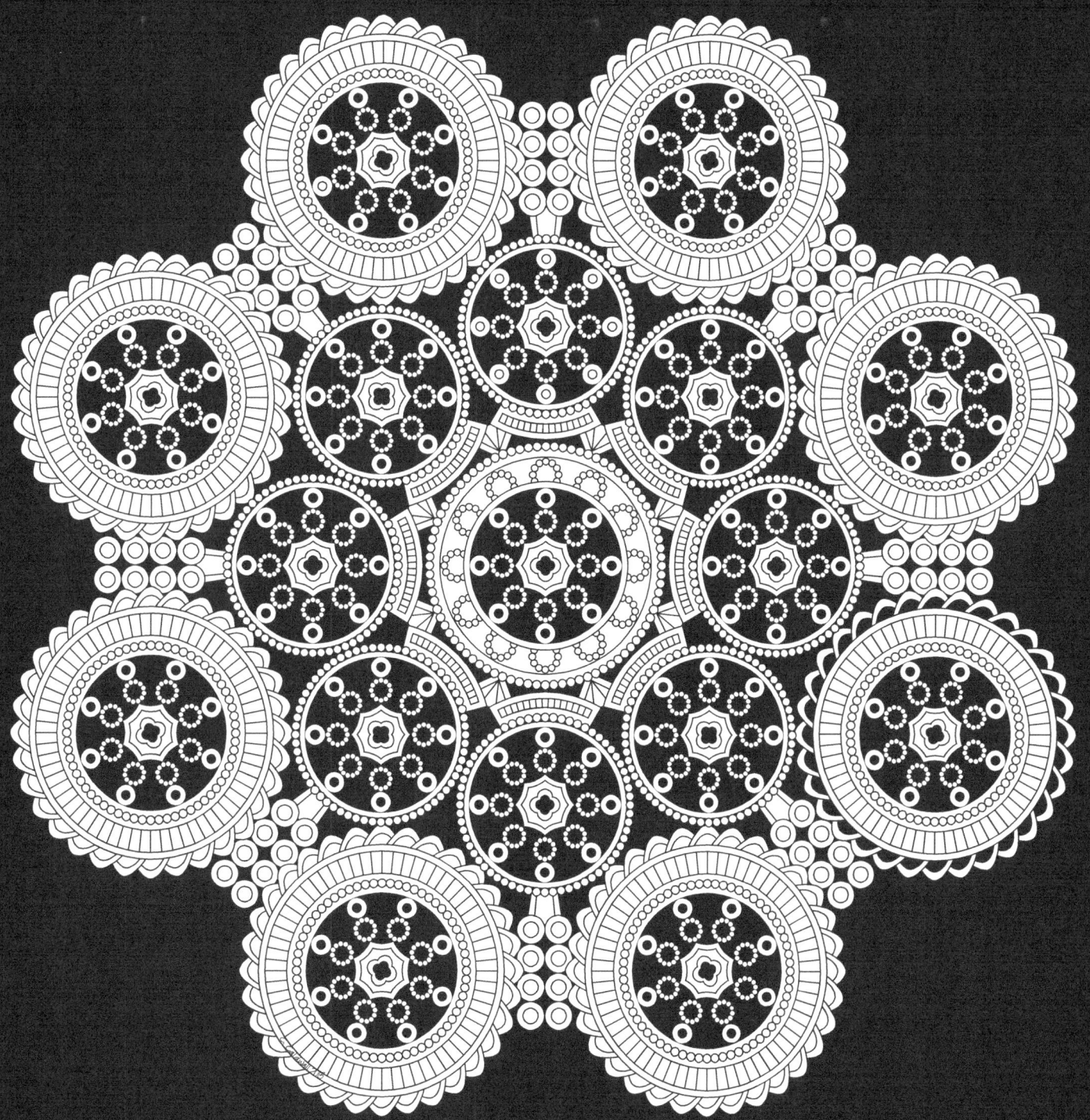

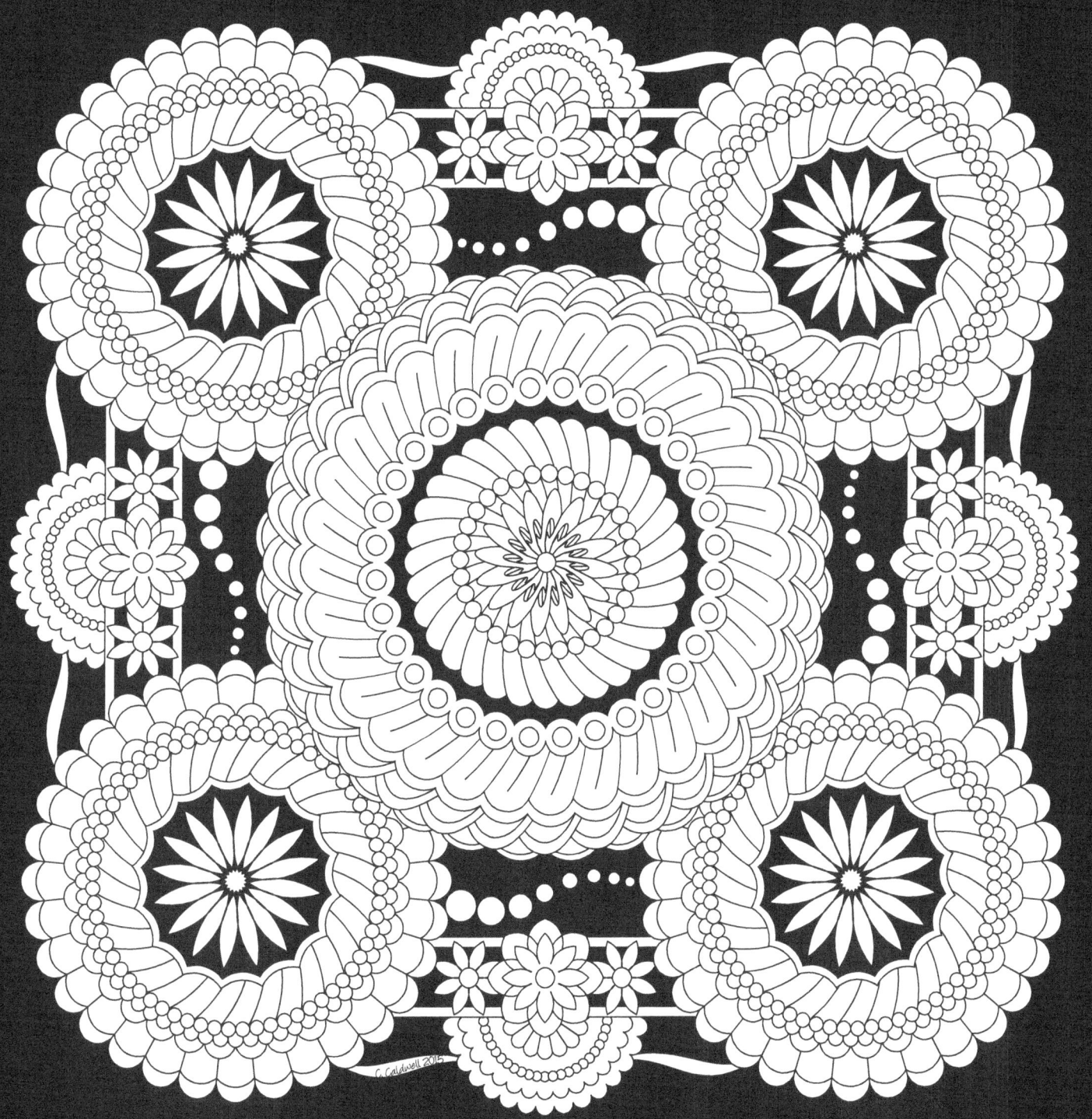

ABOUT THE AUTHOR

Cynthia has always had a passion for drawing. Her original plan was to become a graphic designer, but she lost her way in college and ended up with a degree in computer science. After many years doing software design and development and being out of touch with her creative side, she decided to switch gears. She left the corporate world and began dabbling in web site design and development. But when her daughter was born, her creative vibe came back with a vengeance!

Her daughter inherited her creative genes, and the two of them began exploring the world of arts & crafts together. They enjoy doing projects they find on-line and also inventing their own, so much so that Cynthia decided to start a blog to share these projects with others. So in 2015, she created Yet Another Mom Blog. One of her early blog posts was about coloring books for adults. As she was writing it, she thought "I could do that!" and she created her first official coloring page. She received such positive feedback that she began drawing more coloring pages, which she made available on her blog.

During the summer of 2015, she decided to try to sell some individual coloring pages, and Yet Another Mom Shop on Etsy was opened. Her true passion is hand-drawn intricate scenes and Zentangle®-inspired patterns, which is very time-intensive. She would like to publish a coloring book of these drawings... someday. But she also loves creating repeating patterns and abstract coloring pages (it's that other analytical and OCD side of her), so she decided to begin her publishing career with this *Simple Symmetry* book series.

When she isn't drawing, she writes for her blog, does the occasional freelance consulting job, and she also helps her partner run his IT consulting business. In her little spare time, she loves gardening, sewing, and... coloring!

Visit her blog at YetAnotherMomBlog.com for free coloring page downloads and coloring tips, along with other articles on crafts, DIY, sewing, gardening, cooking and more.

You can also find her on:

Facebook: www.facebook.com/yetanothermomblog
Pinterest: www.pinterest.com/caldcyn
Twitter: www.twitter.com/yamomblog
E-mail: cynthia@yetanothermomblog.com

Feel free to use the following blank sheets to try out colors on this paper, test for bleed, or cut out and use as a protective sheet between the coloring pages (potentially important if you are using wet markers).

PROTECTIVE SHEET/NOTES

PROTECTIVE SHEET/NOTES

www.ingramcontent.com/pod-product-compliance
Lightning Source LLC
Chambersburg PA
CBHW080230180526
45158CB00008BA/2373

* 9 7 8 0 9 9 6 8 6 3 8 0 3 *